First World War
and Army of Occupation
War Diary
France, Belgium and Germany

48 DIVISION
143 Infantry Brigade
Royal Warwickshire Regiment
1/6th Battalion-Territorial
1 March 1915 - 31 October 1917

WO95/2755/2

The Naval & Military Press Ltd
www.nmarchive.com
Published in association with The National Archives

Published by

The Naval & Military Press Ltd

Unit 10 Ridgewood Industrial Park,

Uckfield, East Sussex,

TN22 5QE England

Tel: +44 (0) 1825 749494

www.naval-military-press.com

www.nmarchive.com

This diary has been reprinted in facsimile from the original. Any imperfections are inevitably reproduced and the quality may fall short of modern type and cartographic standards.

© Crown Copyright
Images reproduced by permission of The National Archives, London, England, 2015.

Contents

Document type	Place/Title	Date From	Date To
Heading	1/6th Bn Royal Warwicks March 1913-Oct 1917		
Heading	48th Division 143rd Infy Bde 1-6th Bn Roy. Warwicks Mar 1915-1917 Oct		
Heading	War Diary 1/6th Battn. The Royal Warwickshire Regiment. March 1915		
War Diary	Bayencourt	01/01/1916	03/01/1916
War Diary	Fonquevillers	04/01/1916	16/01/1916
War Diary	Kelvedon	01/03/1915	22/03/1915
War Diary	Le Havre	23/03/1915	24/03/1915
War Diary	Cassel Oudezeele	25/03/1915	28/03/1915
War Diary	Bailleul	28/03/1915	31/03/1915
Miscellaneous	Battalion Operation Orders Nos. 1 & 2.		
Operation(al) Order(s)	Operation Order No. 1 by Lt Col E Martineau V.D. Commanding 1/6th R. War R.	27/03/1915	27/03/1915
Operation(al) Order(s)	Operation Order No. 2 by Lieut Colonel E Martineau V.D. Commanding 1/6th R. War Regt	31/03/1916	31/03/1916
Heading	143rd Inf. Bde 48th Div. War Diary 1/6th Battn. The Royal Warwickshire Regiment.April 1915		
War Diary	Armentieres	01/04/1915	06/04/1915
War Diary	Bailleul	07/04/1915	11/04/1915
War Diary	Point 63 (Petit Pont)	12/04/1915	12/04/1915
War Diary	Point 63	13/04/1915	16/04/1915
War Diary	Douve Trenches	16/04/1915	20/04/1915
War Diary	Jonesville	21/04/1915	23/04/1915
War Diary	Douve Trenches	24/04/1915	28/04/1915
War Diary	Petit Pont	29/04/1915	30/04/1915
Heading	143rd Inf. Bde 48th Div. War Diary 1/6th Battn. The Royal Warwickshire Regiment. May 1915		
War Diary	Petit Pont	01/05/1915	01/05/1915
War Diary	Douve Trenches	02/05/1915	06/05/1915
War Diary	Jonesville	07/05/1915	12/05/1915
War Diary	Douve Trenches	13/05/1915	16/05/1915
War Diary	Petit Pont	17/05/1915	20/05/1915
War Diary	Douve Trenches	21/05/1915	24/05/1915
War Diary	Jonesville	25/05/1915	28/05/1915
War Diary	Douve Trenches	29/05/1915	31/05/1915
Heading	143rd Inf. Bde. 48th Div. War Diary 1/6th Battn. The Royal Warwickshire Regiment. June 1915		
War Diary	Douve Trenches	01/06/1915	01/06/1915
War Diary	Petit Pont	02/06/1915	05/06/1915
War Diary	Douve Trenches	06/06/1915	09/06/1915
War Diary	Petit Pont	10/06/1915	10/06/1915
War Diary	Centre Section	11/06/1915	15/06/1915
War Diary	Ploegsteert	16/06/1915	24/06/1915
War Diary	Bailleul	25/06/1915	25/06/1915
War Diary	Vieux-Berquin	26/06/1915	26/06/1915
War Diary	Norrent-Fontes	27/06/1915	27/06/1915
War Diary	Auchel	28/06/1915	30/06/1915
Heading	Battalion Operation Orders Nos. 4.5,6,7.8 & 9.		

Operation(al) Order(s)	Operation Order No. 4 by Lieut Colonel F.O. Wethered V.D. Commanding 1/6th Battalion The Royal Warwickshire Regt	10/06/1916	10/06/1916
Operation(al) Order(s)	1/6th R. War R Operation Order No. 5.	16/06/1916	16/06/1916
Operation(al) Order(s)	1/6th R. War R Operation Order No. 6	19/06/1915	19/06/1915
Operation(al) Order(s)	Operation Order No. 7.	25/06/1915	25/06/1915
Operation(al) Order(s)	Operation Order No. 8	26/06/1915	26/06/1915
Operation(al) Order(s)	Operation Order No. 9	27/06/1915	27/06/1915
Heading	143rd Inf. Bde. 48th Div. War Diary 1/6th Battn. The Royal Warwickshire Regiment. July 1915		
War Diary	Auchel	01/07/1915	12/07/1915
War Diary	Houchin	13/07/1915	16/07/1915
War Diary	Auchel	17/07/1915	18/07/1915
War Diary	Beauquesne	19/07/1915	19/07/1915
War Diary	Courcelles	20/07/1915	21/07/1915
War Diary	Hebuterne	22/07/1915	25/07/1915
War Diary	Courcelles	26/07/1915	31/07/1915
Miscellaneous	Battalion Operation Orders Nos. 10,11,12,13,14 & 15		
Operation(al) Order(s)	1/6 Battalion Royal Warwickshire Regiment Operation Order No. 10	12/07/1915	12/07/1915
Operation(al) Order(s)	1/6 Battalion Royal Warwickshire Regiment. Operation Order No. 11.	16/07/1915	16/07/1915
Operation(al) Order(s)	1/6 Battalion Royal Warwickshire Regiment Operation Order No. 12	17/07/1915	17/07/1915
Operation(al) Order(s)	1/6th Battalion Royal Warwickshire Regiment Operation Order No. 13	20/07/1915	20/07/1915
Operation(al) Order(s)	1/6 Battalion Royal Warwickshire Regiment Operation Order No. 14	21/07/1915	21/07/1915
Operation(al) Order(s)	1/6 Battalion Royal Warwickshire Regiment Operation Order No. 15.	30/07/1915	30/07/1915
Heading	143rd Inf. Bde. 48th Div. War Diary 1/6th Battn. The Royal Warwickshire Regiment. August 1915		
War Diary	Courcelles	01/08/1915	07/08/1915
War Diary	Trenches	08/08/1915	15/08/1915
War Diary	Courcelles	16/08/1915	25/08/1915
War Diary	Bois De Warnemont	26/08/1915	30/08/1915
War Diary	Sarton	31/08/1915	31/08/1915
Miscellaneous	Battalion Operation Orders Nos,17,19,20,21 & 22.		
Operation(al) Order(s)	Operation Order No. 17	07/08/1915	07/08/1915
Operation(al) Order(s)	1/6 Battalion Royal Warwickshire Regiment Operation Order No. 19	22/08/1915	22/08/1915
Operation(al) Order(s)	1/6 Battalion Royal Warwickshire Regiment Operation Order No. 20	25/08/1915	25/08/1915
Operation(al) Order(s)	1/6 Battalion Royal Warwickshire Regiment Operation Order No. 21	30/08/1915	30/08/1915
Operation(al) Order(s)	1/6 Battalion Royal Warwickshire Regiment Operation Order No. 22	01/09/1915	01/09/1915
Heading	143rd Inf. Bde. 48th Div. War Diary 1/6th Battn. The Royal Warwickshire Regiment. September 1915		
War Diary	Sarton	01/09/1915	02/09/1915
War Diary	Chateau La Haie	03/09/1915	03/09/1915
War Diary	La Haie and fonquevillers	04/09/1915	06/09/1915
War Diary	Sector L	07/09/1915	10/09/1915
War Diary	Bavencourt	11/09/1915	14/09/1915
War Diary	Sector L	15/09/1915	18/09/1915
War Diary	Fonquevillers and Lahnie	19/09/1915	22/09/1915

War Diary	Sector L	23/09/1915	26/09/1915
War Diary	Bavencourt	27/09/1915	30/09/1915
Miscellaneous	Battalion Operation Orders Nos. 23 & 24.		
Operation(al) Order(s)	1/6 Battalion Royal Warwickshire Regiment. Operation Order No. 23	06/09/1915	06/09/1915
Operation(al) Order(s)	1/6 R. War. R. Operation Order No. 24	23/09/1915	23/09/1915
Heading	143rd Inf. Bde. 48th Div. War Diary 1/6th Battn. The Royal Warwickshire Regiment. October 1915		
War Diary	Sector L Trenches	01/10/1915	08/10/1915
War Diary	Fonquevillers & La Haie	09/10/1915	16/10/1915
War Diary	Trenches	17/10/1915	24/10/1915
War Diary	Bavencourt	25/10/1915	31/10/1915
Miscellaneous	Appendices		
Miscellaneous	1/6th. R.War.R.	06/11/1915	06/11/1915
Miscellaneous	1/6th Batt. Royal Warwickshire Regiment.	17/10/1915	17/10/1915
Heading	143rd Inf. Bde. 48th Div. War Diary 1/6th Battn. The Royal Warwickshire Regiment. November 1915		
War Diary	Fonquevillers	01/11/1915	09/11/1915
War Diary	Fonquevillers & La Haie	10/11/1915	17/11/1915
War Diary	Fonquevillers	18/11/1915	25/11/1915
War Diary	Bavencourt	26/11/1915	30/11/1915
Heading	143rd Inf. Bde. 48th Div. War Diary 1/6th Battn. The Royal Warwickshire Regiment. December 1915		
War Diary	Bavencourt	01/12/1915	01/12/1915
War Diary	Fonquevillers	02/12/1915	26/12/1915
War Diary	Bayencourt	27/12/1915	31/12/1915
Miscellaneous	1/6th R Warwick Regt	25/03/1916	25/03/1916
War Diary	Bayencourt	01/01/1916	03/01/1916
War Diary	Fonquevillers	04/01/1916	28/01/1916
War Diary	Bayencourt	29/01/1916	31/01/1916
War Diary	Fonquevillers	17/01/1916	28/01/1916
War Diary	Bayencourt	29/01/1916	31/01/1916
Miscellaneous	1/6 R War Regt Feb 1916 Vol XII		
War Diary	Bayencourt	01/02/1916	04/02/1916
War Diary	Fonquevillers	05/02/1916	29/02/1916
Miscellaneous	1/6 R Warwick Regt Vol XIII March 1916		
Operation(al) Order(s)	1/6th Battalion Royal Warwickshire Regiment. Operation Order No. 26.	03/03/1916	03/03/1916
War Diary	Bayencourt	01/03/1916	03/03/1916
War Diary	Souastre	04/03/1916	07/03/1916
War Diary	Fonquevillers	08/03/1916	31/03/1916
Miscellaneous	Memorandum.	11/03/1916	11/03/1916
Miscellaneous	1st R Warwick Regt	02/03/1916	02/03/1916
Miscellaneous	1/6 R Warwick Regt Vol XIII April 1916		
Operation(al) Order(s)	1/6th Battalion The Royal Warwickshire Regiment. Operation Order No. 27	25/04/1916	25/04/1916
War Diary	Souastre	01/04/1916	08/04/1916
War Diary	Fonquevillers	09/04/1916	25/04/1916
War Diary	Souastre	26/04/1916	30/04/1916
Miscellaneous	D.A.G. 3rd Echelon	02/06/1916	02/06/1916
War Diary	Souastre	01/05/1916	01/05/1916
War Diary	Fonquevillers	02/05/1916	05/05/1916
War Diary	Couin	06/05/1916	07/05/1916
War Diary	Courcelle	08/05/1916	09/05/1916
War Diary	Authie	10/05/1916	10/05/1916
War Diary	Gezaincourt	11/05/1916	23/05/1916

War Diary	Couin	24/05/1916	26/05/1916
War Diary	Authie	27/05/1916	27/05/1916
War Diary	Gazaincourt	28/05/1916	30/05/1916
War Diary	Couin	31/05/1916	31/05/1916
Operation(al) Order(s)	1/6th Battalion The Royal Warwickshire Regiment Operation Order No. 28.	01/05/1916	01/05/1916
Operation(al) Order(s)	Operation Orders No. 29 By Lieut. Colonel W.H. Franklin Commanding 1/6th Battalion The Royal Warwickshire Regiment.	04/05/1916	04/05/1916
Operation(al) Order(s)	1/6 Battalion Royal Warwickshire Regt Operation Order No. 31	31/05/1916	31/05/1916
Operation(al) Order(s)	1/6th Battalion Royal Warwickshire Regiment Operation Order No. 30.	24/05/1916	24/05/1916
War Diary	N Sailly	01/06/1916	07/06/1916
War Diary	Trenches	08/06/1916	12/06/1916
War Diary	Beauval	13/06/1916	22/06/1916
War Diary	Vauchelles	23/06/1916	24/06/1916
War Diary	Beaussart	25/06/1916	25/06/1916
War Diary	Mailly Maillet	26/06/1916	30/06/1916
Operation(al) Order(s)	Operation Order No. 34	21/06/1916	21/06/1916
Operation(al) Order(s)	Operation Order No. 35 Issued By Lieut Col W.H. Franklin Commanding 1/6th R. Warwickshire Regt	22/06/1916	22/06/1916
Operation(al) Order(s)	Operation Order No. 36 Issued By Lieut Col W.H. Franklin Commanding 1/6th Royal Warwickshire Regiment	25/06/1916	25/06/1916
Miscellaneous	Reference Operation Order No. 34.	26/06/1916	26/06/1916
Operation(al) Order(s)	Operation Order No. 37 Issued By Lieut. Col. W.H. Franklin Commanding 1/6 Royal Warwickshire Regiment.	25/06/1916	25/06/1916
Operation(al) Order(s)	Operation Order No. 38 By Lieut. Col. W.H. Franklin Commanding 1/6 R. War. R.	26/06/1916	26/06/1916
Operation(al) Order(s)	Operation Order No. 39 By Lieut. Col. W.H. Franklin Commanding 1/6 R. War. R.	28/06/1916	28/06/1916
Miscellaneous	Amendments To Operation Order No. 39.	30/06/1916	30/06/1916
Operation(al) Order(s)	1/6th Royal Warwickshire Regt. Operation Order No. 31.	30/05/1916	30/05/1916
Miscellaneous	Additions & Amendments To Operation Order No. 34		
Operation(al) Order(s)	1/6th Battalion Royal Warwickshire Regt. Operation Order No. 33	07/06/1916	07/06/1916
Miscellaneous	Appendices		
Heading	143rd Inf. Bde. 48th Div. War Diary 1/6th Battn. The Royal Warwickshire Regiment. July 1916		
War Diary	Mailly	01/07/1916	02/07/1916
War Diary	Couin	03/07/1916	12/07/1916
War Diary	Albert	13/07/1916	19/07/1916
War Diary	Bouzincourt	20/07/1916	23/07/1916
War Diary	Aveluy	24/07/1916	26/07/1916
War Diary	Boisselle	27/07/1916	28/07/1916
War Diary	Maison Rolland	29/07/1916	31/07/1916
Miscellaneous	Battalion Operation Order No. 40		
Operation(al) Order(s)	Operation Order No. 40 Q. C. 1/6th R. War R.	03/07/1916	03/07/1916
Heading	143rd Brigade. 48th Division 1/6th Battalion Royal Warwickshire Regiment August 1916		
War Diary	Maison Rolland	01/08/1916	08/08/1916
War Diary	Gezaincourt	09/08/1916	09/08/1916
War Diary	Lealvillers	10/08/1916	13/08/1916

War Diary	Bouzincourt	14/08/1916	15/08/1916
War Diary	Ovillers	16/08/1916	20/08/1916
War Diary	Bouzincourt	21/08/1916	22/08/1916
War Diary	Ovillers	23/08/1916	26/08/1916
War Diary	Bouzincourt	27/08/1916	27/08/1916
War Diary	Varennes	28/08/1916	28/08/1916
War Diary	Warnemont	29/08/1916	31/08/1916
Operation(al) Order(s)	Operation Order No. 42 By Lt. Col F Q Danielsen Commanding 1/6th R War R.	18/08/1916	18/08/1916
Operation(al) Order(s)	Operation Order No. 41 By Lt. Col. F.Q Danielsen Commanding 1/6th R. War Regt.	13/08/1916	13/08/1916
Heading	143rd Infantry Bde 48th Division 1/6th. Royal Warwickshire Regt. September 1916		
War Diary	Warnemont	01/09/1916	01/09/1916
War Diary	Vauchelles	02/09/1916	10/09/1916
War Diary	Gezaincourt	11/09/1916	17/09/1916
War Diary	Prouville	18/09/1916	27/09/1916
War Diary	Mondecourt	29/09/1916	29/09/1916
War Diary	Bayencourt	30/09/1916	03/10/1916
War Diary	Chateau La Haie	04/10/1916	04/10/1916
War Diary	St Amand	05/10/1916	11/10/1916
War Diary	Hebuterne	12/10/1916	15/10/1916
War Diary	Stamand	16/10/1916	19/10/1916
War Diary	Grande Roullecourt	20/10/1916	24/10/1916
War Diary	Baizieux	25/10/1916	25/10/1916
War Diary	Becourt	26/10/1916	26/10/1916
War Diary	Mametz	27/10/1916	31/10/1916
Operation(al) Order(s)	Operation Order No. 43 By Lieut. Colonel F. G. Danielsen Commanding 1/6 R. War. Regt.	11/10/1916	11/10/1916
Operation(al) Order(s)	1/6 Royal Warwickshire Regt. Operation Order No. 44	20/10/1916	20/10/1916
War Diary	Albert	01/11/1916	02/11/1916
War Diary	Fricourt	03/11/1916	08/11/1916
War Diary	Martinpuich	09/11/1916	11/11/1916
War Diary	Lesars	12/11/1916	14/11/1916
War Diary	Fricourt	15/11/1916	24/11/1916
War Diary	Martinpuich	25/11/1916	28/11/1916
War Diary	Le Sars	29/11/1916	30/11/1916
Heading	War Diary Of 1/6th Bn. Royal Warwickshire Regt. From 1st December, 1916 To 31st December 1916		
War Diary	Le Sars	01/12/1916	02/12/1916
War Diary	Contalmaison	03/12/1916	06/12/1916
War Diary	Martinpuich	07/12/1916	08/12/1916
War Diary	Le Sars	09/12/1916	10/12/1916
War Diary	Contalmaison	11/12/1916	13/12/1916
War Diary	Becourt	14/12/1916	14/12/1916
War Diary	Millencourt	15/12/1916	31/12/1916
Operation(al) Order(s)	Operation Order No. 45 By Lieut. Colonel F.G Danielsen, Commdg 1/6th R. War Regt	09/11/1916	09/11/1916
Operation(al) Order(s)	Operation Order No. 46 By Lieut Col. F.G. Danielsen Commdg 1/6th R War. Regt.	05/12/1916	05/12/1916
Operation(al) Order(s)	Operation Order No. 47 Lt Col F.G. Danielsen Commanding 1/6th R War R.	08/12/1916	08/12/1916
Operation(al) Order(s)	Operation Order No. 48 By Lt. Col. F.G. Danielsen Commdg. 1/6th R. War. Regt	13/12/1916	13/12/1916
Operation(al) Order(s)	Operation Order No. 49 By Lt. Col. F.G. Danielsen Commdg.1/6th R. War. Regt.	14/12/1916	14/12/1916

Operation(al) Order(s)	Operation Order No. 50 By Major W.M Pryor Commdg 1/6th R. War Regt,	27/12/1916	27/12/1916
Heading	War Diary 1/6th R Warwickshire Rgt 1 Jan 1917-31st Jan 1917		
War Diary	Warloy	01/01/1917	08/01/1917
War Diary	Liercourt	09/01/1917	27/01/1917
War Diary	Mericourt	28/01/1917	31/01/1917
Operation(al) Order(s)	Operation Order No. 51 By Major W.M. Pryor, Commdg. 1/6th R.War.Regt.	06/01/1917	06/01/1917
Operation(al) Order(s)	Operation Order No. 52 By Major W.M. Pryor, Commdg, 1/6th R.War.Regt.	07/01/1916	07/01/1916
Operation(al) Order(s)	Operation Order No. 53 By Lt. Col. F.G. Danielsen, D.S.O. Commdg. 1/6th R. War. Regt.	26/01/1917	26/01/1917
Heading	War Diary Of 1/6th Bn. R. Warwickshire Regt. From 1st Feb. To 28th Feb. 1917.		
War Diary	Cappy	01/02/1917	01/02/1917
War Diary	Biaches	02/02/1917	09/02/1917
War Diary	Eclusier	00/02/1917	00/02/1917
War Diary	Biache	10/02/1917	13/02/1917
War Diary	Willikind	14/02/1917	19/02/1917
War Diary	Biache	20/02/1917	25/02/1917
War Diary	Eclusier	26/02/1917	28/02/1917
Operation(al) Order(s)	Operation Order No. 56 By Lt. Col. F.G. Danielsen, D.S.O. Commdg. 1/6th R, War. Regt.	10/02/1917	10/02/1917
Heading	War Diary Of 1/6th Bn. R. Warwickshire R 1st To 31st March 1917		
War Diary	Eclusier	01/03/1917	07/03/1917
War Diary	Biache	08/03/1917	13/03/1917
War Diary	Eclusier	14/03/1917	17/03/1917
War Diary	Mereaucourt Wood	18/03/1917	24/03/1917
War Diary	Peronne	25/03/1917	26/03/1917
War Diary	Bussu	27/03/1917	27/03/1917
War Diary	Saulcourt	28/03/1917	28/03/1917
War Diary	Grebaussart	29/03/1917	31/03/1917
Operation(al) Order(s)	Operation Order No. 56 By Lt. Col. F.G. Danielsen, D.S.O., Commdg. 1/6th R. War. Regt.	06/03/1917	06/03/1917
Operation(al) Order(s)	Operation Order No. 58 By Lt. Col. F. G. Danielsen, D.S.O. Commdg 1/6th R. War. Regt.	28/03/1917	28/03/1917
Operation(al) Order(s)	Operation Order No. 59 By Lt Col. F.G. Danielsen D.S.O. Commdg 1/6th R. War.R.	08/03/1917	08/03/1917
War Diary	Saulcourt	01/04/1917	01/04/1917
War Diary	Epehy	02/04/1917	02/04/1917
War Diary	Grebaussart Wood	03/04/1917	03/04/1917
War Diary	Templeux	04/04/1917	06/04/1917
War Diary	Villers Faucon	07/04/1917	12/04/1917
War Diary	Peiziere	14/04/1917	17/04/1917
War Diary	Chaufours Wood	18/04/1917	21/04/1917
War Diary	Templeux	22/04/1917	29/04/1917
War Diary	Peronne	30/04/1917	30/04/1917
Operation(al) Order(s)	Operation Order No. 59 By Lt. Col F G. Danielsen D S O	16/04/1917	16/04/1917
Miscellaneous	Addition To O.O 40	16/04/1917	16/04/1917
Miscellaneous	Operation Order No. 59 By Lieut. Col F. G. Danielsen, D.S.O. Commdg 1/6 R. War. Regt.	14/04/1917	14/04/1917
Operation(al) Order(s)	Operation Order No. 60 By Lieut. Col. F. G. Danielsen, D.S.O. Commdg, 1/6 R. War. Regt.	20/04/1917	20/04/1917

Operation(al) Order(s)	Operation Order No. 61. By Major W.C.C. Gell, M.C., Commdg 1/6th R. War. R.	28/04/1917	28/04/1917
Operation(al) Order(s)	Operation Order No. 62 By Lt. Col. F.G. Danielsen, D.S.O., Commdg. 1/6th R. War. Regt	29/04/1917	29/04/1917
Heading	War Diary Of 1/6th Bn. R War. R. From 1st May 1917 To 31st May 1917		
War Diary	Eclusier	01/05/1917	02/05/1917
War Diary	Peronne	03/05/1917	11/05/1917
War Diary	Letransloy	12/05/1917	12/05/1917
War Diary	In The Line	13/05/1917	20/05/1917
War Diary	Lebucquire	21/05/1917	28/05/1917
War Diary	In The Line	29/05/1917	31/05/1917
Heading	War Diary Of 6th Royal Warwickshire Regiment. From 1st June To 30th June, 1917		
War Diary	In The Line	01/06/1917	05/06/1917
War Diary	Lebucquiere	06/06/1917	13/06/1917
War Diary	In Line	14/06/1917	21/06/1917
War Diary	Lebucquiere	22/06/1917	22/06/1917
War Diary	Fremicourt	23/06/1917	29/06/1917
War Diary	Gomiecourt	30/06/1917	30/06/1917
Heading	War Diary Of 1/6th Bn. Royal Warwickshire Regt. From 1st July To 31st July, 1917.		
War Diary	Gomiecourt	01/07/1917	01/07/1917
War Diary	Pommier	02/07/1917	19/07/1917
War Diary	Halloy	20/07/1917	22/07/1917
War Diary	St Janster Biezen	23/07/1917	31/07/1917
Operation(al) Order(s)	Operation Order No. 67 By Lt. Col. F G. Danielsen, D.S.O., T.D. Commdg 1/6th Royal Warwickshire Regiment.	01/07/1917	01/07/1917
Operation(al) Order(s)	Operation Order No. 69 By Lt. Col. A.J.N. Bartlett, Commanding 1/6th R. War. Regt.	21/07/1917	21/07/1917
Operation(al) Order(s)	1/6th Royal Warwickshire Regt. Operation Order No. 70.	30/07/1917	30/07/1917
Heading	War Diary Of 1/6th Royal Warwickshire Regiment. From 1st August, To 31st August, 1917		
War Diary	Camp "C" A 30 D	01/08/1917	07/08/1917
War Diary	Camp A30d19	08/08/1917	14/08/1917
War Diary	Dambre Camp St Julien Area	15/08/1917	20/08/1917
War Diary	Regersburg Camp	21/08/1917	27/08/1917
War Diary	St Julien Area	27/08/1917	27/08/1917
War Diary	Regersburg	28/08/1917	28/08/1917
War Diary	Brown Camp	29/08/1917	29/08/1917
War Diary	St Janster Beizen	30/08/1917	31/08/1917
Operation(al) Order(s)	1/6th. Royal Warwickshire Regt. Operation Order No. 72.	14/08/1917	14/08/1917
Operation(al) Order(s)	1/6th Battn Royal Warwickshire Regt. Operation Order No. 71	01/08/1917	01/08/1917
Heading	War Diary Of 1/6th Royal Warwickshire Regiment. From 1st September, To 30th September 1917.		
War Diary	St Janter Biezen	01/09/1917	16/09/1917
War Diary	Louches	17/09/1917	29/09/1917
War Diary	Dambre Camp	30/09/1917	30/09/1917
Miscellaneous	Operation Order By Lt. Col. W.M. Pryor D.S.O. Commanding 1/6th Royal Warwickshire Regiment.	29/09/1917	29/09/1917
Heading	War Diary Of 1/6th Royal Warwickshire Regiment. From 1st October, To 31st October, 1917		

War Diary	Dambre Camp	01/10/1917	02/10/1917
War Diary	Hebuterne	03/10/1917	03/10/1917
War Diary	Assembly Trenches	04/10/1917	04/10/1917
War Diary	Captured Positions	05/10/1917	06/10/1917
War Diary	Langemarke Line	07/10/1917	08/10/1917
War Diary	Irish Farm	09/10/1917	09/10/1917
War Diary	Siege Camp	10/10/1917	10/10/1917
War Diary	Poperinghe	11/10/1917	14/10/1917
War Diary	Mount St Eloi	15/10/1917	16/10/1917
War Diary	In The Line	17/10/1917	27/10/1917
War Diary	Mount St Eloi	28/10/1917	31/10/1917
Miscellaneous	1/6th Royal Warwickshire Regt. Operation Order No. 74a	13/10/1917	13/10/1917
Operation(al) Order(s)	Operation Order No. 74 by Lieut Col Tom Pryor D.S.O. Commdg 1/6 Bn R War R.	02/10/1917	02/10/1917
Operation(al) Order(s)	1/6th Bn. Royal Warwickshire Regt. Operation Order No. 76.	18/10/1917	18/10/1917
Map	Map		
Heading	1/5th Bn Warwick Regt Feb 1916 Vol XII		
Heading	1/6 R Warwick Regt Vol XI January 1916		

16th Bn
Royal
Warwicks

March 1915 — Oct 197

48TH DIVISION
143RD INFY BDE

1-6TH BN ROY. WARWICKS
MAR 1915-MAR 1919
1917 OCT

To 1 THLN

143rd Inf.Bde.
48th Div.

Battn. disembarked
Havre from England
23.3.15.

WAR DIARY

1/6th BATTN. THE ROYAL WARWICKSHIRE REGIMENT.

M A R C H

1 9 1 5

Attached:

Battn. Operation
Orders Nos. 1 & 2.

Army Form C. 2118.

WAR DIARY
or
INTELLIGENCE SUMMARY.

(Erase heading not required.)

No R. Iron R.   January 1916

Instructions regarding War Diaries and Intelligence Summaries are contained in F.S. Regs., Part II. and the Staff Manual respectively. Title pages will be prepared in manuscript.

Place	Date	Hour	Summary of Events and Information	Remarks and references to Appendices
(Wimereux)	1		In Reserve	9 A.M.
"	2		Piquet	9 A.M.
"	3		Reserve	Draft of 16 O.R. / 2 O.R.	9 A.M.
(Loughinishe?)	4		Relieved 15th R. Iran Regt in trenches — 115 Bde on right — 118 2nd Iron R. on left.	9 A.M.
"	5		In Trenches	9 A.M.
"	6		Trenches	9 A.M.
"	7		Trenches	9 A.M.
"	8		Trenches	9 A.M.
"	9		Trenches	9 A.M.
"	10		Trenches	144th relieved 115th Bde on our right.	9 A.M.
"	11		Trenches	2/Lt A.C. Lindsay joined for duty.	9 A.M.
"	12		Trenches	2/Lt R.B. Pyper & 2/Lt W.A. Montrezgame for duty.	9 A.M.
"	13		Relieved by 15th R. Iron R. HQrs & 2 Companies Garrison of FONQUEVILLERS	9 A.M.
"	14		In Support	Major J.E. Dixon transferred to Brigade Res. 2 Companies to LA HAIE	9 A.M.
"	15		In Support		9 A.M.
"	16		In Support	2/Lt. E.B. Rippon joined for duty.	8 A.M.

1/5R. War R

Army Form C. 2118.

WAR DIARY
or
INTELLIGENCE SUMMARY.
(Erase heading not required.)

Hour, Date, Place	Summary of Events and Information	Remarks and references to Appendices
March 1st 1915 KELVEDON	Training	PJS
2 " "	"	PJS
3 " "	"	PJS
4 " "	"	PJS
5 " "	Sunday Training	PJS
6 " "	"	PJS
7 " "	"	PJS
8 " "	"	PJS
9 " "	"	PJS
10 " "	"	PJS
11 " "	"	PJS
12 " "	Sunday Training	PJS
13 " "	"	PJS
14 " "	"	PJS
15 " "	"	PJS
16 " "	"	PJS
17 " "	"	PJS
18 " "	" Capt W H Franklin (Newfoundland Contingent) attached for duty	PJS
19 " "	Sunday	PJS
20 " "	Right ½ Bn. left KELVEDON at 1.50 AM	PJS Details to be left at Been brought
21 " "	Left ½ Bn " " " 3.50 AM Right " " arrived SOUTHAMPTON - 8.0 AM	1st Reinforcement left behind at KELVEDON
22 " "	Left " " " " - 10.0 AM Strength 31 Officers (including 1 A.C.) 997 Other Ranks Battalion Embarked about 6.0 PM Left SOUTHAMPTON about 8.0 PM	

1/6 R Wm. R
WAR DIARY
INTELLIGENCE SUMMARY.
(Erase heading not required.)

Army Form C. 2118.

Place	Date MARCH	Hour	Summary of Events and Information	Remarks and references to Appendices
LE HAVRE	23/15	3:30 AM	Battalion arrived at LE HAVRE. Disembarked & marched to Rest Camp.	R.J
"	24/15	8:0 AM	Left HAVRE in 1 Train. 3 men left in Hospital. 1 Horse Shot.	R.J
"		2:20 PM	Detrained	
CASSEL	25/15	8:30 AM	Arrived by Route March. Accommodated in Billets.	R.J
OUDEZEELE		1:30 PM		
"	26/15	—	Training	R.J
"	27/15	—	Training	R.J
"	28/15	7:30 AM	Left by Route March Route	R.J
BAILLEUL	"	1:30 PM	Arrived. Accommodated in Billets	R.J
"	29/15	5:0 PM	Found 4 Officers 125 Other Ranks for Trench digging in the vicinity of NEUVE EGLISE (Fire and Support Trenches -3'9"x 3' with 9" Command. Communication Trenches -5'x 3' with bank on both sides. Length 250 yards in all)	R.J
"	30/15	5:0 AM	Found 5 officers 250 Other Ranks for Trench digging in vicinity of NEUVE EGLISE (Dimension of works as above for 29th inst. Length about 500 yards)	R.J
"	—	6:0 PM	Found 10 Officers 425 Other Ranks for Trench digging in vicinity of DRANOUTRE (Fire and Support Trenches -3'x 2'6" at top +2' at bottom with 1'6" Command. Communication R.J Trenches -5'x 3' with bank on both sides. Length about 700 yards)	R.J
"	31/15	—	In Billets.	R.J

Pr. Davidson Left
Regt 1/6R Was R

BATTALION OPERATION ORDERS NOS. 1 & 2.

17

Operation Order No 1
by
Lt. Col E. Martineau V.D   Copy No 2
Commanding 1/6 R War. R
Ref Map   OUDEZEELE
Belgium 5A   27. 3. '15
Scale 1/100.000

1. The Battalion will march to BAILLEUL Tomorrow

2. The Battalion will parade ready to march at 7.30 AM. Dress marching order without Packs. Baggage etc. will be packed according to instructions issued to OC Companies & Quartermaster. Baggage of Headquarter party will be stacked outside the MAIRIE by 6.0 AM Tomorrow — the Transport officer will arrange for a waggon to take this.
   1 NCO per company will report at the MAIRIE at 5.0 AM to conduct busses to companies.

3. All ranks will carry the balance of tomorrows ration

Issued at 3.50 PM
Copy No 1 Filed
  "   " 2 War Diary   R. Davidson Capt.
  "   " 3 OC A Co   Adjt 1/6 R War R
  "   " 4 " B "
  "   " 5 " C "
  "   " 6 " D "
  "   " 7 O/C Transport

OPERATION ORDER No. 2. by
LIEUT. COLONEL E MARTINEAU V.D.   Copy No 2
COMMANDING 1/6TH R. WAR. REGT.

Ref Map   Headquarters,
Belgium La   31-3-15
1/100,000

1. The battalion will march to billets in
ARMENTIERES tomorrow.
2. The battalion will parade on the battalion
Alarm Post ready to march off at 12.0 noon.
1st. Line Transport (less 2 S.A.A.Carts and
Pack animals) will be brigaded. Machine Guns
will be brigaded.
All blankets, stores, etc., are to be stacked
outside the Quartermaster's Stores by 9.0 A.M.
All officers' Kits are to be stacked outside
the officers' Mess by 10.30 A.M.

Issued at
Copy 1, Filed.   Copy 2, War Diary.
Copy 3, O.C. "A" Coy. Copy 4, O.C. "B" Coy.
Copy 5, O.C. "C" Coy. Copy 6, O.C. "D" Coy.
Copy 7, Transport officer. Copy 8, M.G.Officer.

                    (Signed) P. V. Davidson,
                    Captain & Adjutant,
                    1/6th. R. War. R.

143rd Inf.Bde.
48th Div.

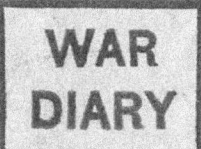

1/6th BATTN. THE ROYAL WARWICKSHIRE REGIMENT.

A P R I L

1 9 1 5

Army Form C. 2118.

1/6R.War.R
WAR DIARY
or
INTELLIGENCE SUMMARY.
(Erase heading not required.)

Instructions regarding War Diaries and Intelligence Summaries are contained in F. S. Regs., Part II. and the Staff Manual respectively. Title pages will be prepared in manuscript.

Place	Date	Hour	Summary of Events and Information	Remarks and references to Appendices
ARMENTIÈRES	1:4:15	4:30 PM	Battalion arrived from BAILLEUL by march route. Accommodated in Billets. Attached to 17th Inf Bde.	R.W
	2:4:	7:30 PM	Found working party of 2 companies for 16th I.B. Communication Trenches dug in vicinity of ARMENTIÈRES. (Dimensions. - 3' × 6' with Earth on both sides)	R.W
		10:30 PM	A storm	R.W
	3:4:	7:50 PM	A and C companies went into Trenches for Tour of Instruction. A company attached to 3rd Rifle Brigade – C company to 1st R.W. Fusiliers.	R.W
	4:4:	7:50 PM	B and D companies relieved A and C companies in Trenches – A and C cos: return to Billets.	R.W
	5:4:	9:30 PM	B company returned to Billets	R.W
	6:4:	1:30 AM	D company returned to Billets.	R.W
		1:15 PM	Battalion handed to march to BAILLEUL	R.W
		4:15 PM	Battalion arrived at BAILLEUL. Accommodated in Billets	R.W
BAILLEUL	7:4		Training	R.W
	8:4		"	R.W
	9:4		"	R.W
	10:4		"	R.W
	11:4		"	R.W
POINT 63 (PETIT PONT)	12:4		Left BAILLEUL 5.0 P.M. Arrived PETIT PONT about 8.0 P.M. Accommodated in Billets about Point 63 in Support to 1/5 R.War.R in Trenches. (Brigade having taken over area occupied by 10th I.B) Found 2 Platoons to occupy 2nd Line of Trenches at 1st Barricade on MESSINES – ARMENTIÈRES road. 2 Platoons return at dawn daily.	R.W

1577 Wt.W10791/1773 500,000 1/15 D.D.&L. A.D.S.S./Forms/C. 2118.

Army Form C. 2118.

WAR DIARY
1/6 R Works
or
INTELLIGENCE SUMMARY.

(Erase heading not required.)

Instructions regarding War Diaries and Intelligence Summaries are contained in F. S. Regs., Part II. and the Staff Manual respectively. Title pages will be prepared in manuscript.

Place	Date	Hour	Summary of Events and Information	Remarks and references to Appendices
Point 63	13.4.15		Found 2 Platoons as for 12th inst. for 1st Barricade from 8.0 P.M. Fike Square. Also Working Parties. Strength 400 Officers and Other Ranks.	P.W
"	14.4		As for 13th	P.W
"	15.4		As for 14th	P.W
"	16.4	7.55 PM	Paraded to Take over Trenches from 1/5 R.War.R	P.W
"	"	10.30 PM	Trenches Taken over.	P.W
Douve TRENCHES	17.4		In Trenches. No 2788 Pte Croft. E killed. Taken off strength	P.W
"	18.4		2 Other Ranks Wounded	P.W
"	19.4		2 Other Ranks Wounded	P.W
"	20.4		Other Ranks taken off strength	P.W
"	20.4	9.0 PM	Relieved by 1/5 R War R. Arrived at hutments JONESVILLE 12 midnight	P.W
JONESVILLE	21.4		Working Party 350 men found for R.E. 1 Other Ranks killed. Struck off Strength	P.W
"	22.4		Working Party 350 men found for R.E 2 Other Ranks Wounded.	P.W
"	23.4		Working Party as for 22.4	P.W
Douve TRENCHES	24.4	10.30 PM	Relieved 1/5 R War R in Trenches	P.W
"	25.4		In Trenches	P.W
"	26.4		" "	P.W
"	27.4		" " 3 Other Ranks Wounded	P.W

Army Form C. 2118.

WAR DIARY
or
INTELLIGENCE SUMMARY.
(Erase heading not required.)

Instructions regarding War Diaries and Intelligence Summaries are contained in F. S. Regs., Part II. and the Staff Manual respectively. Title pages will be prepared in manuscript.

Place	Date	Hour	Summary of Events and Information	Remarks and references to Appendices
DOUVE Trench	28.4		Relieved by 1/5 R Welsh R.	P/W
PETIT PONT	29.4		In billets. Found working party of 600	P/W
" "	30.4		" " " 2 other Ranks wounded	P/W
			Pte Davidson late P&O TS	
			for OC 1/6 R. Welsh R	

143rd Inf.Bde.
48th Div.

WAR DIARY

1/5th BATTN. THE ROYAL WARWICKSHIRE REGIMENT.

M A Y

1 9 1 5

Army Form C. 2118.

WAR DIARY 1/6 R War R
or
INTELLIGENCE SUMMARY.

(Erase heading not required.)

Instructions regarding War Diaries and Intelligence Summaries are contained in F. S. Regs., Part II. and the Staff Manual respectively. Title pages will be prepared in manuscript.

Place	Date	Hour	Summary of Events and Information	Remarks and references to Appendices
PETIT PONT	1.5.15		In billets. Found working party of 600	Rw
DOUVE TRENCHES	2.5.15		Relieved 1/5 R War R	Rw
"	3.5.15		In Trenches. Casualties 1 Other Ranks wounded.	Rw
"	4.5.15		" " 1 Officer (Lt C E Partridge) and 2 O.R. wounded	Rw
"	5.5.15		" " 1 O.R. killed 1 O.R. wounded 2/Lt R.C. Doan joined for duty	Rw
"	6.5.15		" " 1 O.R. killed 2 O.R. wounded. Relieved by 1/5 R War R	Rw
JONESVILLE	7.5.15		In Divisional Reserve in Hutments	Rw
"	8.5.15		" " " "	Rw
"	9.5.15		" " " "	Rw
"	10.5.15		" " " "	Rw
"	11.5.15		Lt. Col. Wartman T.D. assumed command of the Bn.	Rw
"	12.5.15		England. Major J.E. Dixon T.D. assumed command of the Bn.	Rw
DOUVE TRENCHES	13.5.15		Relieved 1/5 R War R. Other Ranks 1 killed 2 wounded.	Rw
"	14.5.15		In Trenches. Casualties Officers 1 wounded (Lt. E.W. Forbes)	Rw
"	15.5.15		In Trenches Casualties Other Ranks 3 killed 14 wounded. Relieved by 1/5 R War R	Rw
"	16.5.15		In Trenches Casualties Other Ranks 1 Died of wounds Other Ranks 1 wounded	Rw
PETIT PONT	17.5.15		Found working parties trenches & widening line by night. Casualties Other Ranks 1 wounded	Rw
"	18.5.15			Rw
"	19.5.15		Relieved 1/5 R War R in Trenches	Rw
"	20.5.15			Rw

Army Form C. 2118.

1/8R wa R

WAR DIARY
or
INTELLIGENCE SUMMARY.
(Erase heading not required.)

Instructions regarding War Diaries and Intelligence Summaries are contained in F. S. Regs., Part II. and the Staff Manual respectively. Title pages will be prepared in manuscript.

Place	Date	Hour	Summary of Events and Information	Remarks and references to Appendices
Douve Trenches	21.5		Casualties. Other Ranks 1 wounded	Ps.d.
"	22.5		" " " 1 killed. 2 wounded. Lt. Col. F.O. Withers Jones resumed command of Bt.	P.d.
"	23.5		" " " 1 wounded.	P.d.
"	24.5		" " " 1 wounded. Relieved by 1/5 R wan R	P.d.
Jonesville	25.5		In Huttments	P.d.
"	26.5		" "	P.d.
"	27.5		" "	P.d.
"	28.5		" " Relieved 1/5 R war R in Trenches. 2/Lt. J.B. HARGREAVE to hospital.	P.d.
Douve Trenches	29.5		Casualties. Other Ranks 2 killed	P.d.
"	30.5		in Trenches	
"	31.5		1 Squadron Glasgow Yeomanry and 50 all Ranks Motor Machine Gun Battery attached for Instruction.	P.d.
			Casting of the Battalion Major J.W.G. Lock Otho Packton	Enr.

P. Davidson Capt.
Adjt 1/8 R wan R

143rd Inf.Bde.
48th Div.

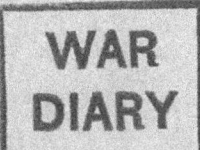

1/6th BATTN. THE ROYAL WARWICKSHIRE REGIMENT.

J U N E

1 9 1 5

Attached:

Battn. Operation
Orders Nos. 4 to 9.

Army Form C. 2118.

1/6R War R
WAR DIARY
or
INTELLIGENCE SUMMARY.
(Erase heading not required.)

Instructions regarding War Diaries and Intelligence Summaries are contained in F.S. Regs., Part II. and the Staff Manual respectively. Title pages will be prepared in manuscript.

Place	Date	Hour	Summary of Events and Information	Remarks and references to Appendices
DOUVE Trenches	1.6.15		Casualties. Other Ranks 1 killed. 2/Lt R.L. LOWE and 4 other Ranks wounded. Relieved by 1/5 R War R.	R.d.
PETIT PONT	2.6.15		Occupied Subsidiary Line. Casualties. O.R. 1 killed.	R.d. R.d
"	3.6.15		Found working parties. Subsidiary Line occupied by 1 company only.	R.d.
"	4.6.15			R.d.
"	5.6.15		Relieved 1/5 R War R in Trenches.	
Douve Trenches	6.6.15		In Trenches.	R.d
"	7.6.15		In Trenches. Dispositions altered. Nos 65 and 64 Trenches evacuated. Nos 36-40 occupied. Casualties. Other Ranks 1 wounded (since died of wounds)	R.d
"	8.6.15		In Trenches.	R.d
"	9.6.15		Relieved by 1/5 R War R.	R.d
PETIT PONT	10.6.15		In billets.	R.d
CENTRE SECTION	11.6.15		Occupied CENTRE SECTION of line as Divisional Troops. (Trenches 32 - 35 inclusive).	R.d R.d
"	12.6.15		In Trenches	
"	13.6.15		In Trenches. Trenches damaged by enemy in front of No 32 Trench. Slight damage to parapet. No attack. Been exploded on side of craters occupied about 10.0 p.m. by party under Lt. GREENER and Corpl. Canadians. Other Ranks 2 wounded.	R.d
"	14.6.15	3.15 AM	Communication established to No. 32 Trench. Casualties. Other Ranks 1 killed.	
"	15.6.15		In Trenches. Casualties. Other Ranks 1 Killed. Relieved by 1/7 R War R. Went into billets about PLOEGSTEERT in Brigade Reserve.	R.d

Army Form C. 2118.

1/4 R. War. R

WAR DIARY
or
INTELLIGENCE SUMMARY.
(Erase heading not required.)

Instructions regarding War Diaries and Intelligence Summaries are contained in F. S. Regs., Part II. and the Staff Manual respectively. Title pages will be prepared in manuscript.

Place	Date	Hour	Summary of Events and Information	Remarks and references to Appendices
Hubrik PLOEGSTEERT	16.6.15		In Billets. Capt. A/S TURNER rejoined Bn from duty with 48th Div'n Staff. 3 companies 7th NORFOLKS attached for instruction.	Par
"	17.6.15		In Billets.	Par
"	18.6.15		In Billets.	Par
"	19.6.15		Relieved 1/5 R. War. R in RIGHT and CENTRE subsections of line. Instruction of 7th NORFOLKS completed. Casualties. Other Ranks 1 wounded.	Par
"	20.6.15		In Trenches. Casualties. Other Ranks 1 killed.	Par
"	21.6.15		In Trenches. Casualties. Other Ranks 1 killed + 4 wounded.	Par
"	22.6.15		In Trenches. Casualties. Other Ranks 3 wounded.	Par
"	23.6.15		Relieved by 1/5 R. War. R. Casualties. Other Ranks 1 killed.	Par
"	24.6.15		In Billets. Billets at BAILLEUL (in billets). Taken over by 7th E. SURREYS	Par
BAILLEUL	25.6.15		Marched to BAILLEUL (in billets).	Par
VIEUX-BERQUIN	26.6.15		Marched to VIEUX-BERQUIN (in billets)	Par
NORRENT-FONTES	27.6.15		Marched to NORRENT-FONTES via MERVILLE - (in billets) Transferred to IV Corps.	Par
AUCHEL	28.6.15		Marched to AUCHEL (in billets)	Par
AUCHEL	29.6.15		In Billets.	Par
AUCHEL	30.6.15		In Billets. Training.	Par

R. Stainson Lieut.
Adjt 1/4 R. War. R

30/6/15

BATTALION OPERATION ORDERS NOS. 4, 5, 6,
7, 8 & 9.

SECRET   OPERATION ORDER No. 4. by   Copy 2
LIEUT. COLONEL F.O. WETHERED, V.D.,
COMMANDING 1/6th. BATTALION THE ROYAL WARWICKSHIRE REGT.

June 10. 1915.

INFORMATION   I.   The 145th. Brigade will take over LEFT SECTION
                    of line from the 143rd. Brigade on 11th. June,
                    1 battalion 143rd. Brigade will relieve 1 battalion
                    145th. Brigade in CENTRE SECTION of line
                    The 1/6th. Bn. R. War. R. will be detached from
                    143rd. Brigade for this purpose and will become
                    Divisional Troops.

DISPOSITIONS   II   The trenches to be taken over from 1 battalion
                    145th. Brigade will be occupied as follows :-

               D Company   1 Platoon in Trench No. 32
                           1 Platoon in support.
                           2 Platoons in No. 32 Support Trench
                     and   (FORT BOYD)

               A Company   Trenches Nos. 33 & 34.

               B Company   2 Platoons in Trench No. 35.
                           1 Platoon in No. 35 Support Trench
                             at ST YVES.
                           1 Platoon in ROTTEN ROW (ST YVES)

               C Company   2 Platoons in Subsidiary line near
                             GLOUCESTER HOUSE
                           2 Platoons and Company Headquarters
                             in HUNTERS AVENUE.
                           This company will find by night a
                           post of 1 N.C.O. and 6 Men in
                           MOATED FARM.

               Battalion   GLOUCESTER HOUSE.
               Headquarters

               Machine Guns : As arranged.

TRANSPORT   III The Transport Officer will take over BUCKS REGT.
                    lines at B.3.c.9.8 and 5.4. (Sheet 36).

RATIONS &
TRENCH STORES &c IV Rations will be taken up on pack animals to
                    POOLE'S COTTAGES in MUD LANE under arrangements
                    to be made by the Transport Officer & Quartermaster.
                    Trench Stores will be stored at POOLE'S COTTAGES

Copy No. 1 Filed.
Copy No. 2 War Diary.
Copy No. 3 O.C.A Company
Copy No. 4 O.C.B Company
   No. 5 O.C.C Company.
   No. 6 O.C.D Company   Captain.
         P.M.   Adjutant, 1/6th. R. War. R.

1/6th. R. War. R.,   OPERATION ORDER NO. 5.

Copy 2

15th. June 1915.

I. Line held by 48th. Division is re-distributed into RIGHT and LEFT Sections.
The 143rd. Infantry Brigade will occupy RIGHT Section today.

II. The 1/6th. R. War. R. will form part of Brigade Reserve and will occupy billets as follows :-
Bn.H.Q. & H.Q. Company at the CONVENT on PLOEGSTEERT - ARMENTIERES road at C.1.a.9.8.
A. Company :- at GRANDE MUNEBUQUE FARM (C.2.a.8.Sheet 36)
B. Company :- at PETITE MUNEBUQUE FARM (C.2.c.0.8.Sheet 36)
C. Company :- at farm just E. of LONDON SUPPORT FARM (in C.2.a Sheet 36)
D. Company :- at farm (U.26.c Sheet 28) on R. WARNAVE.

III. O. C. Companies, will, on arrival at their billets, detail 2 Orderlies to report to Bn. H.Q. (one of these being a Guide). These Orderlies will remain at Bn. H.Q., and be attached to H.Q. Company for rations.

IV. Companies will select Alarm Posts. The position of Bn. Alarm Post will be notified later.
Water bottles are to be kept filled.

V. Transport is at B.7.D.7.6 (Sheet 36)
A G.S.Wagon will be at junction of BUNHILL ROW and STRAND at 4 P.M. for company stores.
A L.G.S.Wagon will be at same place at same time for H.Q. Stores.

VI. Rations and letters will be brought this evening to Bn. H.Q.
O. C. Companies will on arrival at their billets send 1 man (additional to those mentioned above in Order No.III) to conduct ration carts to company billets.
C Company's field kitchen will accompany it, the remaining field kitchens proceeding to join their companies with the ration carts.

(Signed) P. V. Davidson,
Captain & Adjutant,
1/6th. R. War. Regt.

Copy No. 1 Filed
"   " 2 War Diary
"   " 3 A Coy.
"   " 4 B "
"   " 5 C "
"   " 6 D "
"   " 7 H.Q."

Ref. ST YVES 1/10000
RELINGHIEN 1/10000

1/6th. R. WAR. R.   OPERATION ORDER No. 6.   Copy 2

June 19th 1915.

1. The 1/6th. R. War. R. will relieve the 1/5th. R. War. R. in the RIGHT and CENTRE Sub-sections of the line (Trenches 1--19 inclusive) today.

2. DISPOSITIONS

Sub-Section Commander, Capt. H.H.Parkes.
RIGHT Sub-section A and B Companies (Trenches 1--10 inclusive.)

Sub-Section Commander Capt. F.M.Chatterley.
CENTRE Sub-section C and D Companies (Trenches 11--19 inclusive).

The O. C. RIGHT Sub-section will detail 3 Sections for permanent garrison at : S.Pt.2 (C 5 d);   S.Pt.3 (FORT PAUL);   S.Pt.4 (FORT DUDLEY)
The O.C. CENTRE Sub-section will detail 2 Sections for permanent garrison at : S.Pt.7 (LANCASHIRE SUPPORT FARM)

Machine Guns under arrangements to be made by officer in charge.

3. Reliefs will be carried out under arrangements to be made by O.C.Sub-sections at about 6 P.M., commencing as soon as possible after the issue of rations.

4. Rations for A and B Companies will be dumped today at C.7.D.4.8 at 3 P.M. and will be drawn from that point. Rations for C and D Companies will be dumped today at road junction 300 yards N.E. of SALFORD VILLAGE, All spare kits to be sent to Transport farm and Field Kitchens will be sent to dumping posts at 3 P.M., when they will be collected by Transport.
Further instructions as to issue of rations in trenches will be issued.

5. Watercarts will be deposited by night as follows :
1 at ESSEX FARM.   1 at DESPIERRE FARM.

6. Position of Regimental Aid-Post, SUMMERS FARM.

R. Davidson
                                    Captain,
Issued at 12 noon   Adjutant, 1/6th.R.War.R.

By Orderly.

Copy No. 1 Filed
 "   2 War Diary
 "   3 O.C.RIGHT Sub-section
 "   4 O.C.CENTRE Sub-section.
 "   5 O.C.Machine Guns
 "   6 O.C.Transport.

1/6th. R. WAR. R.,   OPERATION ORDER No. 7.   Copy 2

Reference   June 25th 1915.
HAZEBROUCK Sheet 5a
BELGIUM 1/100,000

I.   48th. Division will withdraw from its present position in the
     line and will march to VIEUX BERQUIN, - 143rd. Brigade and
     attached troops marching to BAILLEUL on night 25th/26th June,
     when relieved by 7th E.SURREYS about 10 P.M.

II. The Battalion will march to BAILLEUL via ROMARIN and RABOT.

III. Starting Point will be second road bend WEST of cross roads
     PLOEGSTEERT (immediately under S of 5,000) on PLOEGSTEERT -
     ROMARIN road and will be marked by 1 white lamp.
     Companies will assemble at the Starting Point at 10.30 P.M.
     in column of route in following order : A, B, C, & D.
     Machine Gun Section following in rear.
     Each company will send an officer to head of column to report
     when present.
     Each company will leave 1 officer and 1 N.C.O. per platoon
     in billets to hand over to 7th. E.SURREYS - these parties
     rejoining battalion at starting point immediately the relieving
     companies have arrived.

IV. Capt. A.B.Turner and 1 N.C.O. per company will report to
     Staff Captain at 28 RUE DE LILLE, BAILLEUL, at 3 P.M. today
     to arrange billets.

V.   Rations will be at usual dumps at 3 P.M. today.
     Field Kitchens are to be at Ration dumps at 5 P.M.
     Water Carts will be removed at 2 P.M.

VI. Officers' Kits must be stacked on empty ration carts and must
     be at dumps at 3 P.M.
     Headquarters Baggage will be ready stacked at the CONVENT at
     4 P.M.
     Maltese Cart will be at CONVENT at 4.30 P.M., when it will be
     at once loaded and returned to Transport.
     Officers Mess Cart will call for A and B Company's boxes at
     3;30 P.M., and for C and D Company's at 4 P.M.   On no account
     will anything additional to 2 mess boxes per company be placed
     on this cart.
     Dixies (2 per company for officers) may be attached to Field
     Kitchens.

VII. Officers' Chargers will await them at the CONVENT.

VIII. Transport will join the battalion at RABOT.

                                                Captain.
                                Adjutant, 1/6th. R. War. R.
     Issued at
        by orderly.

     Copy No. 1 - Filed.
        "   2 - War Diary.
        "   3 - O.C. A Coy.
        "   4 - O.C. B Coy.
        "   5 - O.C. C Coy.
        "   6 - O.C. D Coy.
        "   7 - M.C. H-Qs Coy.
        "   8 - O.C. Transport.

Copy No. 2

1/6th. R. War. R.,   OPERATION ORDER No. 6

Reference   June 24th. 1915.
HAZEBROUCK &
1/100,000

1. 143rd. Infantry Brigade with attached Divisional troops
   will march to VIEUX BERQUIN tonight.
   Brigade starting point : Road Junction S. or A in
   STEAM MILL on BAILLEUL - VIEUX BERQUIN Road.

2. Companies, etc., will pass the battalion starting point
   (junction of RUE DE CASSEL and RUE DES MOULINS) in the
   following order commencing at 8.15 P.M. :- Signallers,
   B, C, D, A, Companies, Pioneers, Machine Gun Section,
   1st. Line Transport.

3. 2nd. Field Ambulance will join in behind the Brigade at
   Cross roads S. of C in THANCK at 9.40 P.M.

4. The O.C. A Company will detail a reliable N.C.O. *of the Bn.*
   march in rear of the Brigade to bring on any stragglers
   at pace of slowest. Men falling out are to be instructed to wait for this party and on no account to try
   and find their own way.

5. The O.C. Transport will collect all officers' kits at
   once.

6. On arrival at billets companies will send 2 orderlies
   to Battn. Headquarters. This must be done whenever a
   move takes place;

                                        [signature]
                                              Captain
                                    Adjutant, 1/6th.R.War.R.

Issued by orderly at 6 P.M.

Copy No. 1 : Filed
   "   2 : War Diary.
   "   3 : O.C. A Coy.
   "   4 : O.C. B Coy.
   "   5 : O.C. C Coy.
   "   6 : O.C. D Coy.
   "   7 : O.C. A-Qs Coy.
   "   8 : O.C. Transport.

1/6th. R. WAR. REGT., OPERATION ORDER No. 9

Copy No. 2

Reference
HAZEBROUCK 5a
1/100,000

27th. June 1915.

1. 143rd. Infantry Brigade with attached troops will march to HAM-EN-ARTOIS tonight via MERVILLE, ST. VENANT, and GUARBEQUE.

2. Companies, etc., will pass the starting point (road junction immediately under C. of LA RUE DU BOIS) moving towards VERTE RUE in the following order :- Signallers, C, D, A, B, Companies, Machine Gun Section; the leading companies passing the starting point at 8.25 P.M.

3. (a) 1st. Line Transport will follow battalion.
   (b) Supply Wagons will march with battalion.
   (c) Supply column will 'dump' at HAM-EN-ARTOIS at 4.30 P.M. tomorrow.

4. The O.C. "B" Company will detail 1 reliable N.C.O. to march in rear of the column to bring on stragglers of battalion at pace of slowest.
   Men are to be instructed to wait for this party and on no account to try and find their own way.

5. There will be an hour's halt in addition to the usual halts.

6. (a) No parcels are to be carried.
   (b) Singing and smoking are allowed.
   (c) Officers and N.C.O's. responsible for march discipline may occasionally move up and down their commands.
   (d) All horses are to be dismounted at halts.

7. LILLERS is out of bounds.

Captain
Adjutant, 1/6th. R. War. R.

Issued at 6.52 P.M. by orderly

Copy No. 1 : Filed
      " 2 : War Diary.
      " 3 : O.C. A Coy.
      " 4 : O.C. B Coy.
      " 5 : O.C. C Coy.

143rd Inf.Bde.
48th Div.

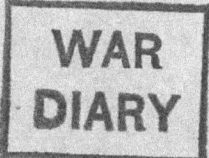

1/6th BATTN. THE ROYAL WARWICKSHIRE REGIMENT.

J U L Y

1 9 1 5

Attached:

Battn. Operation
Orders Nos. 10 to
15.

Army Form C. 2118.

1/8 R Lon R **WAR DIARY**
or
INTELLIGENCE SUMMARY.
(Erase heading not required.)

Instructions regarding War Diaries and Intelligence Summaries are contained in F. S. Regs., Part II. and the Staff Manual respectively. Title pages will be prepared in manuscript.

Place	Date	Hour	Summary of Events and Information	Remarks and references to Appendices
AUCHEL	1.7.15		In Corps Reserve. Training. Capts. I.A. Fyshe, H.G. Parker & J. Rounds invalided	R.W.
"	2		"	R.W.
"	3		"	R.W.
"	4		"	R.W.
"	5		"	R.W.
"	6		"	R.W.
"	7		"	R.W.
"	8		" Lieut route for Sunday & State for War.	R.W.
"	9		"	R.W.
"	10		"	R.W.
"	11		"	R.W.
"	12		Moved to Lillers-Bivouac at HOUCHIN by march route.	R.W.
HOUCHIN	13		In bivouac.	R.W.
"	14		" Casualties. Other Ranks 1 wounded. 2/Lt R.C. Lowe Rejoined for duty	R.W.
"	15		"	R.W.
"	16		Moved to AUCHEL by march route.	R.W.
AUCHEL	17		In huts.	R.W.
"	18		Marched to LILLERS. Entrained there and train detrained at MONDICOURT PAS, moved by march route to BEAUQUESNE	R.W.
BEAUQUESNE	19		In bivouac.	R.W.

1577 Wt. W10791/1773 500,000 1/15 D. D. & L. A.D.S.S./Forms/C. 2118.

Army Form C. 2118.

1/6 R br R

WAR DIARY
or
INTELLIGENCE SUMMARY.

(Erase heading not required.)

Instructions regarding War Diaries and Intelligence Summaries are contained in F. S. Regs., Part II. and the Staff Manual respectively. Title pages will be prepared in manuscript.

Place	Date	Hour	Summary of Events and Information	Remarks and references to Appendices
COURCELLES	20.7		Moved from BEAUQUESNE by march route. In Bivouac.	Rw
"	21.7		Took over Trenches N. and E. of HEBUTERNE from French (93rd Regiment)	Rw
HEBUTERNE	22.7		In Trenches. Casualties Other Ranks 1 wounded	Rw
"	23.7		In Trenches. Casualties Other Ranks 3 wounded.	Rw
"	24.7		In Trenches. Casualties Other Ranks 1 wounded. Relieved by 1/5 R br R.	Rw
"	25.7		Moved to Billets in COURCELLES	Rw
COURCELLES	26.7		In Brigade Reserve	Rw
"	27.7		" "	Rw
"	28.7		Worked in trenches in Reserve. Detachment in Brigade Reserve accidentally wounded. 1 Other Ranks	Rw
"	29.7		In Brigade Reserve. Casualties 1 Other Ranks accidentally wounded.	Rw
"	30.7		In Divisional Reserve	Rw
"	31.7		In Divisional Reserve.	Rw

R. Davidson Capt.
Cmdr 1/6 R br R

1577 Wt. W10791/1773 500,000 1/15 ⓒ D. D. & L. A.D.S.S./Forms/C. 2118.

BATTALION OPERATION ORDERS NOS. 10, 11, 12,
        13, 14 & 15.

1/6 BATTALION ROYAL WARWICKSHIRE REGIMENT.

Operation Order No. 40.   Copy No. 2

Reference Sheet No 3   12th. July, 1915.

1. The Brigade marches to billets and bivouacs at HOUCHIN tonight (Distance about 8 miles)

2. The battalion will pass the starting post (cross roads C28 b & 6) at 7-30 p.m. in the following order C, D, A, B, Machine Gun Section, 1st. Line Transport (and Train if accompanying units)

3. All kits will be handed to the Transport officer by 4-30 p.m.

4. Great coats will be carried in the valise.

5. (1) Rations (except bread) will be carried in the Field Kitchen
   (2) Filled waterbottles will be carried and watercarts will be filled before starting.

                                                        4 30

                        _____ Captain & Adjutant,
                                                1/6 R. War. R.

Issued by orderly at 5.30 p.m.

Copy No. 1 Filed
  "   " 2 War Diary
  "   " 3 O. C. A. Company
  "   " 4 " " B. "
  "   " 5 " " C. "
  "   " 6 " " D. "
  "   " 7 M. G. Section
  "   " 8 Transport
  "   " 9 M. O.

1/6 BATTALION ROYAL WARWICKSHIRE REGIMENT.

Operation Order No. 11.

Copy No. 2

Reference 36 B

July 16th, 1915

1. The Battalion will move to Auchel to-day.

2. The Battalion will parade at 8-15 p.m. on the ground of the present bivouac - D Coy. facing the road on the west side in succession A, B, & C.

3. Grenadier Platoon to march with the battalion.

4. 1st. line Transport immediately in rear of the Battalion.

5. The Transport Officer will draw four boxes of very light ammunition from S. A. A. carts of the 7th. R. War. R. to-day.

6. Great coats to be carried in the packs.

7. O. C. C. Coy. will detail 1 Officer and 1 NCO to collect stragglers.

8. Officer's kits will be collected at the Orderly Room at 5-30 p.m. Kitchens to be ready by 7 p.m.

Issued by orderly at 2.20 p.m.

J. L. Mellor / Capt.

for Captain & Adjutant,

1/6 R. War. R.

Copy No. 1 Filed.
" " 2 War Diary.
" " 3 A Company.
" " 4 B "
" " 5 C "
" " 6 D "
" " 7 M. G. Section
" " 8 Transport.
" " 9 M. O.

1/8 BATTALION ROYAL WARWICKSHIRE REGIMENT

SECRET   Copy No. 2

Ref. 36A & B   Operation Order No. 15.   July 17th. 1916.
1/40,000

1. (1) The Division will move by road and rail to the 3rd. Army Area
       on 18th. July and following days. On arrival it will form part
       of the 7th. Corps which consists of 4th., 48th. and 1 new Division.
   (2) The Battalion will entrain at LILLERS tomorrow at 3.1 p.m.

2. (1) A Company and all horses and vehicles (including Machine Gun
       limbers and supply wagons) of the Battalion will leave AUCHEL
       at 10-0 a.m. tomorrow under arrangements to be made by the O. C.
       A Company. This party must report to Major Dixon at LILLERS
       station at 12 noon tomorrow, marching via RAIMBERT and BURBURE.
   (2) The Battalion (less A Company) will pass A Company's parade ground
       in the following order at 12-1 p.m. : Grenadiers, Signallers,
       B, C, D Companies, Machine Gun Section.
   (3) Headquarters Company (less Machine Gunners and Transport) will
       parade with their Coys.

3.   Major J. R. Dixon V. D. will superintend the entraining and
       detraining of the Battalion.

4. (1) All kits will be sent to the transport by 8 a.m.
   (2) Supply wagons will be fitted with one day's supplies.
   (3) All vehicles will be entrained loaded.
   (4) Forage and buckets for watering horses must be so placed as to
       be readily available during train journey.
   (5) The journey will take about 4 hours.

5.   The O. C. A. Company will detail any loading parties that may
       be required by the Transport Officer before arrival at LILLERS.

       Issued at 7.40 P.M.

       Copy No. 1. Files.
         "   "   2. War Diary.
         "   "   3. O. C. A. Company.
         "   "   4. "   B.   "
         "   "   5. "   C.   "
         "   "   6. "   D.   "
         "   "   7. " Headquarters Company.
         "   "   8. Transport Officer.
         "   "   9. O. C. Grenadiers.

                                          R Davidson Captain,
                                          Adjutant, 1/8 R. War. R.

SECRET.   1/6 BATTALION ROYAL WARWICKSHIRE REGIMENT.
                                                                    Copy No. 2

                            Operation Order No. 13.

Reference AMIENS
        Sheet 1B.
                                                           20th. July, 1915.

1. (a) 48th. Division will relieve 42nd. French Brigade in the
         Trenches N and E of HEBUTERNE on the nights of 20th. and
         21st. July, 1915;   143rd. Brigade will take over right
         section of French line - 145th. Brigade will take over
         left section of French line.

    (b) 143rd. Brigade will be disposed as follows:-

                1/6th. R. War. R. in line on right.
                1/8th. R. War. R. in line on left.
                1/5th. R. War. R. in Brigade reserve.
                1/7th. R. War. R. "   "   "

         The Battalion will take over line from the French
         on night 21/22nd. July, 1915.

2. The Battalion will march to bivouac at COURCELLES today.
    Parade ready to move at 2-55 p.m. The Transport will
    follow the battalion as it passes the Transport field.

3. The O. C. C Company will detail an NCO (with map) to
    march at rear of the battalion to collect stragglers and
    to bring them on at pace of slowest to COURCELLES.

4. All kits will be sent to Transport by 1-0 p.m.

                                              R. Dhunusson
                                                     Captain,
                                         Adjutant, 1/6. R. War. R.

        Issued at 10-15 a.m. by orderly.
        Copy No. 1. Filed.
          "   " 2. R. War Diary.
          "   " 3. O. C. A Company.
          "   " 4.   "   B   "
          "   " 5.   "   C   "
          "   " 6.   "   D   "
          "   " 7.   "   HQ   "
          "   " 8. Transport.

1/C BATTALION ROYAL FUSILIERS REGIMENT.   Copy No. 2

Ref. AMIENS MAP.   Operation Order No. 4.   1st. July,
                                                          1916.

1. The 48th. Division relieves the 22nd. French Brigade in the
   line tonight.

2. The Battalion will relieve the 4??. French Regiment in the
   line tonight.

3. (a) The relief will be carried out by Companies, etc.-
       Companies etc. leaving CAVILLES at 7-0 p.m. in the following
       order:- A - Companies - B - C - D and Headquarter Details.
       An interval of 200 yards must be kept between Companies etc.
   (b) Distribution as follows:-
           Firing Line   A and B Companies
           Support   "   C Company
           Reserve   "   D   "
           At ???????   ?? ??????? ??? ??????
           ???????
   (c) Machine Gun Section will take over French positions
       commencing at 6-30 p.m.

4. Transport will remain at CAVILLES; also R^ts M^t and Details as arranged

5. The M. O. will establish a R. A. Post at HEBUTERNE - with an
   advanced dressing station in the communication trench (as
   used by the French).

6. O. C. Companies and Machine Gun Section will report immediately
   relief is completed.

                                       R. Charlton   Captain,
                                       Adjutant, 1/C R. Fus. R.

Issued at 33. V. R. by orderly.

   Copy No. 1 Files.
    "   "   2 War Diary.
    "   "   3 O. C. A. Company.
    "   "   4   "   " B   "
    "   "   5   "   " C   "
    "   "   6   "   " D   "
    "   "   7   "   Machine Gun Section.
    "   "   8   "   Transport.
    "   "   9   M. O.
    "   " 10 OC Grenadiers

SECRET   1/6 BATTALION ROYAL WARWICKSHIRE REGIMENT.   Copy No. 2

                    Operation Order No. 15.

Reference:-
    Map 1/80,000 AMIENS   July 30th. 1915.

1. 143rd. Infantry Brigade will be relieved by 144th. Infantry
    Brigade today and will become Divisional Reserve.

2. 1/6 R. War. R. will remain at COURCELLES with Transport
    at COIGNEUX.

3. The O. C. Machine Gun Section will remove Machine Guns
    from Trenches, bringing out 3,500 rounds per gun.

4. Grenadier Platoon will move to billets in SAILLY under
    arrangements to be made by O C. Grenadier Company.

                                    R. D_____ Captain,
                                    Adjutant, 1/6 R. War. R.

Issued at 6.25 a.m. by orderly.

        Copy No. 1 Filed.
         "   " 2 War Diary
         "   " 3 O C. A Company.
         "   " 4   "   B   "
         "   " 5   "   C   "
         "   " 6   "   D   "
         "   " 7   "   HQ   "
         "   " 8   "   Grenadiers
         "   " 9   "   Transport.

143rd Inf.Bde.
48th Div.

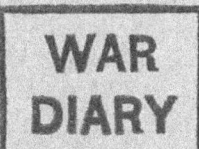

1/6th BATTN. THE ROYAL WARWICKSHIRE REGIMENT.

A U G U S T

1 9 1 5

Attached:

Battn. Operation
Orders Nos. 17, 19,
20, 21 & 22.

Army Form C. 2118.

1/6 R. War. R

WAR DIARY
of
INTELLIGENCE SUMMARY.
(Erase heading not required.)

Instructions regarding War Diaries and Intelligence Summaries are contained in F. S. Regs., Part II. and the Staff Manual respectively. Title pages will be prepared in manuscript.

Place	Date	Hour	Summary of Events and Information	Remarks and references to Appendices
	1915			
COURCELLES	1st Aug.		In Divisional Reserve	R.d
"	2nd "		" " "	R.d
"	3rd "		" " "	R.d
"	4th "		" " "	R.d
"	5th "		" " "	R.d
"	6th "		Relieved 6th GLOUCESTERS in Lieu of HEBUTERNE Trenches	R.d
"	7th "		In Trenches	R.d
Trenches	8th "		In Trenches Casualties Other Ranks 2 accidentally wounded	R.d
"	9th "		In Trenches	R.d
"	10th "		In Trenches	R.d
"	11th "		In Trenches	R.d
"	12th "		In Trenches	R.d
"	13th "		In Trenches Casualties Other Ranks 2 wounded. Major J. Christopher 3/6 R. War. R.	R.d
"	[14th] "		Challenger proceeded to England for duty with 3/6 R. War. R. Other Ranks 3 wounded	R.d
"	14th "		In Trenches Casualties Other Ranks 1 killed 2 wounded. Relieved by	R.d
"	15th "		In Trenches Casualties Other Ranks 1 killed 2 wounded. Relieved by 6th GLOUCESTERS. Returned to Billets at COURCELLES and COLINCAMPS	R.d
COURCELLES	16th "		In Divisional Reserve	R.d
"	17th "		" " "	R.d
"	18th "		" " "	J & M
"	19th "		" " "	J & M
"	20th "		" " "	J & M

Army Form C. 2118.

WAR DIARY 1/6 R.W.R.
or
INTELLIGENCE SUMMARY.
(Erase heading not required.)

Place	Date	Hour	Summary of Events and Information	Remarks and references to Appendices
COURCELLES	21st Aug		In Divisional Reserve 2nd Lieut O.W. Clarke joined	J.2.h
"	22nd		" Armourer Sergt. and 14 other ranks joined	J.2.h
"	23rd		Relieved 6th GLOUCESTERS in Section F HEBUTERNE Trenches. 2nd Lt E.P. Moore joined.	J.1.h
"	24th		In Trenches	J.2.h
"	25th		Relieved by 2nd ESSEX - moved to bivouac in BOIS DE WARNEMONT	J.2.h
BOIS DE WARNEMONT	26th		In Divisional Reserve	J.2.h
"	27th		"	J.2.h
"	28th		"	J.1.h
"	29th		"	J.1.h
"	30th		moved to billets at SARTON	J.1.h
SARTON	31st		"	J.1.h

J.V. Dinwiddie Col.
A/Lt 1/6 R.W.R.

BATTALION OPERATION ORDERS NOS. 17, 19,
20, 21 & 22 .

SECRET   Copy No. 2

1/6 R. War. R.   Operation Order No. 17.

Reference Maps
ARTRES 1/80,000 & Trench Maps   7th. AUGUST 1915.

1. (a) 143rd. Infy Bde will relieve 144th Infy Bde in Trenches today.

   (b) 1/6 R.War. R. will relieve 6th. GLOUCESTERS in portion of
       line 503 exclusive to Trench 33 inclusive.

2.   Companies will be distributed as follows:- take over exact
       dispositions of 6th. GLOUCESTERS.

3. (a) The relief will be carried out independently by Companies
       commencing at 4 p.m., A, C, & D Companies and Machine Gun
       Section via Boyau BAREILEO and Headquarters and B COMPANY via
       CEMETERY.

   (b) Guides for A, C & D Companies will be at point where BAREILEO
       crosses HEBUTERNE - BAILLY road at 4-30 p.m.; guides for B Coy.
       will be at CEMETERY at 4-40 p.m.

   (c) A Company will move to COLINCAMPS via Point 102.

4.   The working party of C Company at LA SIGNY will, on relief
       by 6th. GLOUCESTERS, rejoin their Company.

5. (a) Transport will move to COIGNEUX today.

   (b) O.C. Transport will fetch surplus kits from COLINCAMPS at 2 p.m.
       (at) COIGNEUX at 2-45 p.m.
       1 Limbered wagon will be sent to C & D Companies at 3 p.m. for
       Trench kit and 1 limbered wagon to A & B Coys. at 3 p.m.

   (c) Water carts will be stationed at HEBUTERNE.

   (d) All cookers (except B Coy's which will proceed to HEBUTERNE)
       will rejoin Transport after dinners.

   (e) O.C. Transport will hand over all reserve ammunition to
       6th. GLOUCESTERS.

6.   Rations will be dumped daily at CEMETERY

7.   Reserve N.C.O.'s Teams will rejoin their Coys. on arrival in Trenches.

8.   The Grenadier Platoon will rejoin the Battalion, moving to
       Trenches from BAILLY at 4-30 p.m. via CEMETERY.

9.   The Snipers will parade under Sergeant Griffiths at 3 p.m. at
       COIGNEUX and move to allotted position via CEMETERY at that hour.
       They will be rationed by A Company.

10.   The S.O.S. signal for artillery support is a red followed by
       a green rocket fired from the Trenches and repeated until
       support is received.

Operation Order No. 17 Contd:-

11. O.C. Coys. will report by wire immediately they have relieved and will then send 2 orderlies to Bn. H.Q. for permanent duty.

(Sgd) R. D. Davidson, Captain.

Adjutant, 1/6 B. War. R.

Copy No. 1 Filed
     "   2 War Diary
     "   3 O.C. A Company
     "   4 " B   "
     "   5 " C   "
     "   6 " D   "
     "   7 " M.G. Section
     "   8 " Grenadiers.
     "   9 " Transport.
     " 10 Sergt. Griffiths.

1/6 BATTALION ROYAL WARWICKSHIRE REGIMENT*　　　Copy No. 2

Operation Order No. 19.

Reference Map
AMIENS 1/80,000
and Trench Maps.　　　　　　　　　　　　　　22nd. August, 1915.

1. (a) 143rd. Infy. Bde. will relieve 144th. Infy. Bde. in Trenches tomorrow.

   (b) 1/6 R. War. R. will relieve 6th. GLOUCESTERS.

2. B and C Coys. (C Coy on right and both Coys. with two platoons in fire trench and two platoons in support) will relieve via WAGRAM and JEAN BART, leaving COURCELLES at 10-15 a.m.
   D Coy. (in support) and A Coy. (in reserve) will relieve via WAGRAM - JEAN BART and DUGUESLIN respectively leaving COURCELLES at 2-15 p.m.

3. Signallers, Machine Gun Section and Grenade Platoon will relieve via WAGRAM and JEAN BART, leaving their respective billets at 10-45 a.m.
   Reserve Machine Gun Teams, after providing carrying parties for their guns, will rejoin their Companies.

4. Transport will bivouac at COIGNEUX, taking over Transport lines there at 11 a.m. 23rd. inst.
   O.C. Coys will arrange direct with Transport Officer re carriage of kits and stores required in trenches.

5. Battalion Headquarters will open in Trenches at 3-30 p.m.
   O.C. Coys., M.G. Section and Grenade Platoon will report immediately relief is completed.

　　　　　　　　　　　　　　　　　　　　　　Captain,
　　　　　　　　　　　　　　　　　　Adjutant, 1/6 R. War. R.

Issued at　　　　p.m.

　　　Copy No. 1　Filed
　　　　　　　 2　War Diary.
　　　　　　　 3　O.C. A Company.
　　　　　　　 4　 "　 B　　 "
　　　　　　　 5　 "　 C　　 "
　　　　　　　 6　 "　 D　　 "
　　　　　　　 7　 "　 Transport.
　　　　　　　 8　 "　 M.G. Section
　　　　　　　 9　 "　 Grenade Platoon
　　　　　　　10　Sergt. Higgs.
　　　　　　　11　Quartermaster
　　　　　　　12　M.O.

1/6 BATTALION ROYAL WARWICKSHIRE REGIMENT.   Copy No. 2

Operation Order No. 20

Reference
AMIENS (Sheet 12)
and Trench Map.   25/8/15.

1 (a) The 2nd. Essex will relieve the 1/6 R. War. R. Today.

  (b) The relief will take place about 3-30 p.m.

2   The Battalion on relief will proceed to bivouac at BOIS-de-WARNEMONT via HEBUTERNE-COURCELLES and BUS-LES-ARTOIS.

3   The route of relief will be JEAN BART and DUGUESLIN.

4   Relief of Machine Guns will be completed by 12 noon.

5   Machine Gun limbers will be at CEMETERY, HEBUTERNE by 12 noon. Officers horses, limbered wagons and mess cart at 4 p.m.

6.   Orders respecting moving ammunition and bombs will be issued later.

J L Mellor Captain,
Acting Adjutant, 1/6 R. War. R.

Issued at 6 10 am.

Copy No. 1 Filed
      2 War Diary
      3 O.C. A Company.
      4 "   B   "
      5 "   C   "
      6 "   D   "
      7 "   M.G. Section
      8 Transport Officer.
      9 O.C. Grenade Platoon
    10 M.O.
    11 Quartermaster.

1/6 BATTALION ROYAL WARWICKSHIRE REGIMENT.   Copy No. 2

Operation Order No 21.
                                        30 th. August, 1915.

Reference
AMIENS (Sheet 12)

1. The Battalion will move to billets this afternoon.   All parades
   (including washing) cancelled.

2. Battalion will proceed via AUTHIE to billets at SARTON.

3. Companies and Departments will parade separately on their own
   parade grounds at 4 p.m.

4. They will concentrate on road on south side of BOIS de WARNEMONT
   in following order:- Grenadiers, Signallers, A, C and D Coys.
   Machine Gun Section. by 4-20 p.m.
   B Company will proceed independently on return of parties from
   bathing.
                                 ent
5. Transport will parade independly and join Battalion at road junction
   ¼ mile west of B in BOIS de WARNEMONT.

6. Officers kits and mess boxes to be at Orderly Room by 2-30 p.m.
   Surplus goods to be stacked separately from those urgently needed.

                                        Captain,
                                        Acting Adjutant, 1/6 R. War. R.

Issued at   p.m.

    Copy No. 1 Filed
             2 War Diary
             3 O.C. A Company.
             4   " B   "
             5   " C   "
             6   " D   "
             7   " HQ   "
             8   " Grenade Platoon.
             9 Transport Officer.
            10 Quartermaster.
            11 M.O.

SECRET

1/6 BATTALION ROYAL WARWICKSHIRE REGIMENT.   Copy No 2

Operation Order No. 22

Reference   1st. September 1915.
AMIENS (Sheet 12)

1. (a) 143rd. Infantry Bde. takes over from the French between
       September 2nd. and 4th.

   (b) The 6th. R.War.R. and Grenade Coy. will move to Chateau de la
       Haie on 2nd. inst.

2.   The Battalion will parade at 9-30 a.m. in the following
      order:- Grenadiers, Signallers, B, C, D, A Coys and Machine
      Gun Section.

3.   The head of the column will be in the main street facing S.E.
      at corner of Thievres road.

4.   Cookers will proceed with the Battalion and prepare dinners
      for issue on arrival (about 1-0 p.m.)

5.   The Machine Gun Officer is referred to Bde. Operation Order No 41

6.   The Transport and Q.M. Stores will accompany the Battalion -
      but will break off at BAYENCOURT, where they will be brigaded.

7.   Shoemaker and Armourer must accompany the Battalion.

8.   Officers kits and mess boxes must be stacked at corner of
      the lane leading to Transport Field at 8-0 a.m.

9.   Only Headquarter horses will be allowed at the Chateau de la Haie.

                                            J L Mello /Captain,
Issued at 4 p.m.
                                      Acting Adjutant, 1/6 R.War.R.

      Copy No 1 Filed.
             2   War Diary
             3   O.C. A Company
             4   " B   "
             5   " C   "
             6   " D   "
             7   Machine Gun Officer.
             8   Grenade Officer
             9   Quartermaster.
            10   Transport Officer.

143rd Inf.Bde.
48th Div.

WAR DIARY

1/6th BATTN. THE ROYAL WARWICKSHIRE REGIMENT.

SEPTEMBER

1915

Attached:

Battn. Operation Orders
Nos. 23 & 24.

WAR DIARY
1/6 R War R
INTELLIGENCE SUMMARY.

(Erase heading not required.)

Army Form C. 2118.

Place	Date	Hour	Summary of Events and Information	Remarks and references to Appendices
SARTEN	1st Sept		In Billets.	Nil
"	2nd Sept		Moved to CHATEAU LA HAIE	Nil
CHATEAU LA HAIE	3rd		In Billets	Nil
LA HAIE and FONQUEVILLERS	4th		Headquarters and A and D companies moved to FONQUEVILLERS as garrison of Southern Defences of that village. B and C Coys remaining as garrison of LA HAIE	Nil
"	5th		2 coys and H.Q. 6th BEDFORDS attached for instruction	Nil
"	6th		Relieved 1/5 R War R in Right Section of line (FONQUEVILLERS) 1 company 6th BEDFORDS attached for instruction. Lt. W. MARTINEAU joined for duty. Appointed Signalling Officer	Nil
SECTOR	7th		In Trenches	Nil
"	8th		In Trenches. Casualties other Ranks 1 wounded	Nil
"	9th		In Trenches	Nil
"	10th		Relieved by 1/5 R War R marched to billets at BAYENCOURT In B. de Reserve	Nil
BAYENCOURT	11th			Nil
"	12th		In Brigade Reserve.	Nil
"	13th			Nil
"	14th		Relieved 1/5 R War R in Trenches	Nil

1/6 Rhn. R
WAR DIARY
—or—
INTELLIGENCE SUMMARY.
(Erase heading not required.)

Army Form C. 2118.

Instructions regarding War Diaries and Intelligence
Summaries are contained in F. S. Regs., Part II.
and the Staff Manual respectively. Title pages
will be prepared in manuscript.

Place	Date	Hour	Summary of Events and Information	Remarks and references to Appendices
Potvin L	15th		In Trenches	Ro
"	16th		In Trenches. Casualties, Other Ranks 1 accidentally wounded	Ro
"	17th		In Trenches	Ro / Ro
"	18th		Relieved by 1/5 Rhn. R. H.Qrs + 2 coys to FONQUEVILLERS + 2 coys to LA HAIE	Ro
FONQUEVILLERS and LA HAIE	19th		Lt. W. MacIntosh proceeded for attachment to 4th Div. Signal Co.	Ro / Ro
"	20th		In support. Other Ranks 1 wounded	Ro / Ro
"	21st		"	Ro / Ro
"	22nd		Relieved 1/5 Rhn. R. in Trenches	Ro
Sector L	23rd		In Trenches	Ro
"	24th		In Trenches. Lt. L. N. GREENER and 2/Lt. I. WALKER accidentally wounded	
"	25th		In Trenches 2/Lts. C. Thomas, Davis, R. Rice, J. Balkwill, C. A. Elton and J. G. Cooper joined for duty. 2/Lt. J. WALKER evacuated	Ro
"	26th		Relieved by 1/5 Rhn. R.	Ro
BAYENCOURT	27th		In Brigade Reserve	Ro / Ro
"	28th		" Casualties Other Ranks 1 wounded	Ro
"	29th		"	Ro
"	30th		Relieved 1/5 Rhn. R. in Trenches	Ro

P. Shenton Capt
Adjt 1/6 Rhn R

BATTALION OPERATION ORDERS NOS. 23 & 24.

1/6 BATTALION ROYAL WARWICKSHIRE REGIMENT.   Copy No. 2

SECRET.   Operation Order No 23.

Reference Map   8th. September 1915
AMIENS 1/80,000

1. 1/6 R.War.R. will relieve 1/5 R.War.R. in right section of
   FONQUEVILLERS today.

2. (1) B and C Companies will commence relief at 1-0 p.m. moving
   via communication trench from LA HAIE to FONQUEVILLERS. Guides
   will meet these companies at entrance to FONQUEVILLERS at 1-30 p.m.

   (2) A and B Companies will commence relief as soon as relieved
   by 1/7 R.War.R. at about 2-15 p.m.

   (3) Details will relieve at 1-0 p.m.

3. Cookers etc for B and C Companies will move up after dark.

4. Bombers will join their Companies.

5. O.C. Companies will report as soon as relief is completed
   and will send two orderlies to remain at Headquarters permanently.

                                    ....Captain,
                              Adjutant, 1/6 R. War. R.

Issued at 11.10 a.m.

     Copy No 1 Filed.
            2   War Diary
            3   O.C. A Company.
            4   "   B   "
            5   "   C   "
            6   "   D   "
            7   "   Transport
            8   "   M.G.Section.
            9   Sergeant Major.

S E C R E T.

1/6 R. WAR. R. - OPERATION ORDER No. 24.   Copy No. 2

Reference Maps.
AMIENS Sheet 12
and Trench Map 1/10.000.   23rd September, 1915.

---

1.   Owing to operations in other parts, the general situation by the end of the present week may be such as to enable the 3rd Army to attack the enemy in our front, or take part in a general advance.

2.   The 143rd Infantry Brigade will be prepared (A) To attack the German 1st and 2nd line trenches near the North end of GOMMECOURT Wood, (B) or, leaving about 2 Companies and some machine guns covering its present front, to march to support an attack elsewhere.

    Commencing on the afternoon of 23rd Sept., the Battalion will keep such a constant and sufficient sniping fire directed on all places where the enemy tries to work or move, that further strengthening of any of his lines or repair of damage done by the Artillery will be practically impossible by day or night.

    The Artillery will begin bombarding selected places in the enemy's lines on the afternoon of Sept. 23rd.

    On the afternoon of the 24th Sept., the Artillery will cut the enemy's wire by deliberate fire at selected places and the gaps made will be kept open by night by intermittent gun and rifle fire.

    Every man will go forward with 170 rounds S.A.A. on him - i.e., 1 extra bandolier.

    In the event of an advance, no water other than that carried forward will be drunk until further orders are issued.

Issued at   p.m.
                                              Captain.
                                   Adjutant 1/6 R.War.R.

Copy No. 1.   Filed.
     2.   War Diary.
     3.   O.C., A Company.
     4.   "   B   "
     5.   "   C   "
     6.   "   D   "
     7.   "   M.G.Section.

143rd Inf.Bde.
48th Div.

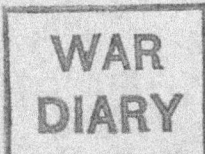

1/6th BATTN. THE ROYAL WARWICKSHIRE REGIMENT.

O C T O B E R

1 9 1 5

Attached:

Appendices.

Army Form C. 2118.

WAR DIARY
or
INTELLIGENCE SUMMARY

1/6 R War R   October 1915

(Erase heading not required.)

Instructions regarding War Diaries and Intelligence Summaries are contained in F. S. Regs., Part II. and the Staff Manual respectively. Title pages will be prepared in manuscript.

Place	Date	Hour	Summary of Events and Information	Remarks and references to Appendices
Hebuterne Trenches	1st		In Trenches	Rw
"	2nd		"	Rw
"	3rd		"	Rw
"	4th		"	Rw
"	5th		"	Rw
"	6th		"	Rw
"	7th		"	Rw
"	8th		Relieved by 1/5 R War R. H.Q. + 2 Coys to FONQUEVILLERS - 2 Coys to LA HAIE	Rw
FONQUEVILLERS & LA HAIE	9th		In Support of FONQUEVILLERS. Casualties other Ranks 5 wounded. 2nd Lieut. N H B BAXTER joined for duty	Rw
"	10th		In Support	Rw
"	11th		In Support	Rw
"	12th		In Support	Rw
"	13th		In Support Casualties OR 1 wounded	Rw
"	14th		In Support	Rw
"	15th		In Support	Rw

Army Form C. 2118.

WAR DIARY

1/6 R War R INTELLIGENCE SUMMARY. October 1915

(Erase heading not required.)

Instructions regarding War Diaries and Intelligence Summaries are contained in F. S. Regs., Part II. and the Staff Manual respectively. Title pages will be prepared in manuscript.

Place	Date	Hour	Summary of Events and Information	Remarks and references to Appendices
FONQUEVILLERS & LA HAYE	16th		Relieved 1/5 R War R in Trenches	R.d.
Trenches	17th		In Trenches	R.d.
"	18th		In Trenches	R.d.
"	19th		In Trenches. H.Q.rs and A and B Coys 13th Bn. R. Irish Rifles attached for Instruction	R.d.
"	20th		In Trenches	R.d.
"	21st		In Trenches. Casualties O.R. 1 wounded	R.d.
"	22nd		In Trenches	R.d.
"	23rd		In Trenches	R.d.
"	24th		Relieved by 1/5 Rotnes R. Moved to Brigade Reserve at BAYENCOURT	R.d.
BAYENCOURT	25th		In Brigade Reserve	R.d.
"	26th		" " "	R.d.
"	27th		" " "	R.d.
"	28th		" " "	R.d.
"	29th		" " "	R.d.
"	30th		" " "	R.d.
"	31st		" " "	J.W.M.

1577 Wt. W10791/1773 500,000 1/15 D. D. & L. A.D.S.S./Forms/C. 2118.

APPENDICES.

Copy No. 2

1/6TH. R. WAR. R.

RELIEF. 17/11/15.

1. Companies will relieve Companies of 1/5 R. War. R. in trenches tomorrow.

2. A and D companies will leave LA HAIE at 11 a.m.

   B and C companies will leave FONQUEVILLERS when relieved by 1/7 R. War. R. about 12 noon.

3. A. company will be in line on the right.
   C. company will be in line on the left.
   B. company will be in support.
   D. company will be in reserve.

   In future A and B companies will always relieve each other. Similarly C and D companies until further orders.

4. Companies will relieve each other in the front line every 24 hours - relief to be completed by 2.30 p.m. daily.

5. Companies in front line will find 2 platoons for protection and 2 platoons for work day and night.

6. The company in Support will carry Rations, R.E. Stores, Water and Ammunition etc. for the Right Company. Similarly the company in Reserve will carry for the Left Company, until further orders.

7. Working hours for working platoons in front line:-
   First Day.   2.30 p.m. - 4. p.m.
                   6.0 p.m. - 12 midnight.

   Second Day   8.0 a.m. - 12 noon.

8. The necessary Transport will call at LA HAIE at 10.15 a.m. and at FONQUEVILLERS at 11.15 a.m.

9. Cookers will be taken to BAYENCOURT by 1/5 R. War. R.

10. Companies will always report immediately relief is complete.

11. O.C. Companies will report in their daily work report the number of yards and nature of wire which has been put out during previous 24 hours.
    NIL reports must be rendered.

12. O.C. Companies will report daily by 3.30 p.m. number of bombs thrown from WEST bombthrower.
    NIL returns not required.

continued.

Relief. 17/11/15. Continued.

13. As the number of returns to be sent to Brigade has been
    greatly increased lately, O.C. Companies are requested
    to be punctual and careful with their reports.

14. Each Company will send an Officer into the trenches early
    tomorrow morning to take over from 1/6 R. War. R.

15. Separate instructions have been issued to M.O.O.

16. Attention is directed to "Distribution of Grenades etc. in
    L. Sector" issued on 13th. inst.

                                            Captain.
                                    Adjutant 1/6 R. War. R.
6/11/15.

Copy No. 1. Filed.
        2. War Diary.
        3. O.C. Detachment at H.Q. 143rd. H.F. Bgde.
        4. O.C. "B" Co.
        5. O.C. "D" Co.
        6. O.C. Transport.
        7. Quartermaster.
        8. M.O.

1/6TH BATT. ROYAL WARWICKSHIRE REGIMENT.

ATTACHMENT OF 13TH BATT. R. IRISH RIFLES.

Reference Map
Sheet 57 D.
1/40.000.

1. Headquarters and A and B Coys. 13th R.I.R., will be attached to this battalion for the following periods.

   HEADQUARTERS ... from 19th - 22nd Oct.
   A and B COYS. ... from 19th - 25th Oct.

2. 2 Platoons, A Coy, 13th R.I.R., will be attached to right Coy. in line from 19th-21st Oct., and 2 Platoons A Coy, 13th R.I.R., to the left Coy in line for the same period.

   2 Platoons, B Coy, 13th R.I.R., will be attached to the Support Coy from 19th-21st Oct, and 2 Platoons B Coy, 13th R.I.R., to the Reserve Coy for the same period.

   On the morning of 22nd October, platoons of A Coy, 13th R.I.R., will change over with platoons of B Coy, 13th R.I.R., under arrangements to be made between O.C., Coys, 13th R.I.R. and 1/6 R.War.R. concerned.

3. O.C.Coys will arrange for 1 guide per Coy to be at the cross roads at J.6.b.13 at 9.55 a.m. on Oct.19th, where they will meet 2 Officers from A Coy, 13th R.I.R. and 2 Officers from B Coy, 13th R.I.R.

   The Company Guides will then conduct Officers, 13th R.I.R., as follows :-

   (1 Officer A Coy,13th R.I.R. to Head Qrs.of A Coy.
   (1 Officer A Coy,13th R.I.R. to Head Qrs.of C Coy.

   (1 Officer B Coy,13th R.I.R. to Head Qrs.of B Coy.
   (1 Officer B Coy,13th R.I.R. to Head Qrs.of D Coy.

   The Officers,13th R.I.R., will then make the necessary arrangements for the arrival and disposition of their Coys.

4. O.C.Coys. will each send a guide on 19th Oct., to meet A and B Coys, 13th R.I.R. at road junction, D 21.b.3.1 at 5.30 p.m., when each guide will conduct 2 Platoons, 13th R.I.R. to their quarters. Head Quarters, 13th R.I.R., will be met at the same place and at the same time by an Officer to be detailed by the O.C. B Coy, 1/6 R. War. R., and conducted to Battalion Head Quarters.

5. O.C.Coys and M.O. will ensure that the personnel, 13th R.I.R., receive thorough instruction in the following :-

   (a) Sentry duty.
   (b) Action on "ALARM" (gas or otherwise)

(2)

     (c) Patrol duty in trenches.
     (d) Wire erection and maintenance.
     (e) Patrolling outside the wire.
     (f) Digging and fatigue duties.
     (g) Listening posts.
     (h) Distribution of rations.
     (j) Bombing and trench mortar work.
     (k) Sniping and observation.
     (l) Evacuation of sick and wounded.
     (m) Relieving.
     (n) Action in case of shell fire.
     (o) Sanitation.
     (p) General trench cunning.
     (q) Machine gun uses and duties.
     (r) Signal service.

6. Transport Officer and Quartermaster will shew the Transport Officer and Quartermaster, 13th R.I.R., everything connected with Transport and Supply duties.

7. The following transport *only* will accompany, 13th R.I.R. to FONQUEVILLERS ;-

        Cookers.
        Water Carts.
        Medical Cart.
        Baggage wagons.

17th October, 1915.
                                            Captain.
                                     Adjutant 1/6 R. WAR.R.

COPY No. 1   Filed.
        2   War Diary
        3   O.C. A Coy.
        4   " B "
        5   " C "
        6   " D "
        7   Transport Officer.
        8   Quartermaster.
        9   M.O.
       10   O.C. A Coy, 13th R.I.R.
       11   O.C. B Coy, 13th R.I.R.

143rd Inf.Bde.
48th Div.

WAR DIARY

1/6th BATTN. THE ROYAL WARWICKSHIRE REGIMENT.

N O V E M B E R

1 9 1 5

Army Form C. 2118.

WAR DIARY
or
INTELLIGENCE SUMMARY.
(Erase heading not required.)

1/6ᵗʰ R War R   November 1915

Place	Date	Hour	Summary of Events and Information	Remarks and references to Appendices
FONQUEVILLERS	1ˢᵗ		Relieved 5ᵗʰ R War R in Trenches – 8ᵗʰ R War R on our left	JLM
"	2ⁿᵈ		In trenches – 1/4ᵗʰ R. J. R. attached for instruction withdrawn	JLM
"	3ʳᵈ			JLM
"	4ᵗʰ		Casualties 1 Officer 2ⁿᵈ/Lt R C Lowe & 1 O.R. wounded	JLM
"	5ᵗʰ			JLM
"	6ᵗʰ		Casualties 1 O.R. wounded	JLM
"	7ᵗʰ			JLM
"	8ᵗʰ		G.O.C. awards 2ⁿᵈ Lt Lowe the Military Cross & No 2041 Sergt E Rott the D C M.	JLM
"	9ᵗʰ		Relieved by 5ᵗʰ R War R. H.Q & 2 Coʸ to Fonquevillers – 2 Coʸ to Chateau LA HAIE	JLM
			2ⁿᵈ Lieut K W BROWN & 1 O.R. joined for duty	
"LA HAIE	10ᵗʰ		In support.	RW
"	11ᵗʰ		"	RW
"	12ᵗʰ		"	RW
"	13ᵗʰ		"	RW
"	14ᵗʰ		"	RW
"	15ᵗʰ		"	RW

Army Form C. 2118.

1/5thBn. R WAR DIARY for November 1915
or
INTELLIGENCE SUMMARY.
(Erase heading not required.)

Instructions regarding War Diaries and Intelligence
Summaries are contained in F. S. Regs., Part II.
and the Staff Manual respectively. Title pages
will be prepared in manuscript.

Place	Date	Hour	Summary of Events and Information	Remarks and references to Appendices
FONQUEVILLERS & LA HAYE	16/11/15		In Support	Pw.
	17th		Relieved 1/5 R War R in Trenches	Pw.
FONQUEVILLERS	18th		In Trenches. 1 Company 12th R. Irish Rifles attached	Pw.
"	19th		In Trenches. Lt. Col. H. Williams 9th Inniskilling Fusiliers attached.	Pw.
"	20th		In Trenches.	Pw.
"	21st		In Trenches.	Pw.
"	22nd		In Trenches. Lt. Col. H. Wilkinson 9th Inniskilling Fusiliers left.	Pw.
"	23rd		In Trenches.	Pw.
"	24th		In Trenches	Pw.
"	25th		Relieved by 1/5 R War R. In Reserve	Pw.
BAYENCOURT	26th		" " "	Pw.
"	27th		" " "	Pw.
"	28th		" " " Draft of 25 Other Ranks arrived from 1st Entrenching Bn.	Pw.
"	29th		" " "	Pw.
"	30th		" " "	Pw.

P.N. Brickman Capt
Actg Yorkman [?]

143rd Inf.Bde.
48th Div.

WAR DIARY

1/6th BATTN. THE ROYAL WARWICKSHIRE REGIMENT.

DECEMBER

1915

Army Form C. 2118.

WAR DIARY

1/6 Rhine R.   December 1915

INTELLIGENCE SUMMARY.

(Erase heading not required.)

Instructions regarding War Diaries and Intelligence Summaries are contained in F. S. Regs., Part II. and the Staff Manual respectively. Title pages will be prepared in manuscript.

Place	Date	Hour	Summary of Events and Information	Remarks and references to Appendices
BAYENCOURT	1st		In Reserve	Res.
	2nd		In Reserve	Res.
FONQUEVILLERS	3rd		Relieved 1/5 Rhine R in Trenches 145th Bde on Right – 1/8 Rhine R on left	Res.
"	4th		In Trenches	Res.
"	5th		In Trenches	Res.
"	6th		In Trenches. 144th Bde relieves 145th Bde on our Right.	Res.
"	7th		In trenches	J.d.m
"	8th		In trenches – HQ & 2 Cos of 17th Manchesters attached	J.d.m
"	9th		In trenches – Col C Moss 13th Cheshires attached.	J.d.m
"	10th		In trenches	J.d.m
"	11th		Relieved by 1/5th R War R. – HQ & 2 Companies to FONQUEVILLERS – 2 Cos to LA HAIE	9d.m
			(11th Batt 17th Manchesters attached.	
"	12th		In Support.	9d.m
"	13th		Support – Col C Moss left	J.d.m
"	14th		In Support. 115th Bde relieves 144th Bde. – 17th Manchesters left.	J.d.m
"	15th		In Brigade Support	9d.m
"	16th		In Brigade Support	J.d.m

1/6 R. War. R. WAR DIARY or INTELLIGENCE SUMMARY.

Army Form C. 2118.

December 1915

Place	Date	Hour	Summary of Events and Information	Remarks and references to Appendices
FONQUEVILLERS	Dec 17th		In Support	9th m
"	18th		In Support	9th m
"	19th		Relieved 1/5 R.War.R. in Trenches. 145th Bde on Right. 1/8 R.War.R. on Left. H.Q. & A. Co. of 19th Liverpools attached. Draft of 35 O.R. arrived from 1st Entrenching Batt's	9th m
"	20		In Trenches	9th m
"	21		In Trenches	9th m
"	22		In Trenches 144th Bde relieves 145th Bde on our right	9th m
"	23		In Trenches	9th m
"	24		In Trenches Casualties 1 O.R wounded - 19th Liverpools left	9th m
"	25		In Trenches	9th m
"	26		In Trenches	9th m
Bayencourt	27		Relieved by 1/5th R.War.R. Moved to Brigade Reserve at Bayencourt	9th m
"	28		In Reserve 145 Bde relieves 144th Bde	9th m
"	29		In Reserve	9th m
"	30		In Reserve	9th m
"	31		In Reserve	9th m

J.C. Wetherall Lt Col R.
Comm. 1/6 R.War.R.

O.C.
1/6 R Warwick Regt

CONFIDENTIAL

A.G.'s OFFICE AT THE BASE
CENTRAL REGISTRY
20 MAR 1916
C.R. No. 8700/275

Your original War Diary for October 1915 was received in this Office & forwarded to War Office 17.11.15.

War Diary for January 1916 is still required in this Office please.

H. Yates Capt
for D.A.G.

GHQ
3rd Echelon
25. 3. 1916

Army Form C. 2118.

/16th R War R.

WAR DIARY
or
INTELLIGENCE SUMMARY.

Jan 1916

XLVIII

(Erase heading not required.)

Place	Date	Hour	Summary of Events and Information	Remarks and references to Appendices
BAYENCOURT	Jan 1		In Reserve	JLM
"	2		In Reserve — Draft of 16 O R	JLM
"	3		In Reserve " " 2 O R	JLM
FONQUEVILLERS	4		Relieved 1/5th R War R in trenches 1/15th R War R on left	JLM
"	5		In Trenches 1/15th Bde on right — 1/6th R War R on left	JLM
"	6		In Trenches	JLM
"	7		In Trenches	JLM
"	8		In Trenches	JLM
"	9		In Trenches 4th relieves 143rd Bde on our right	JLM
"	10		In Trenches 2nd Lt. B.G. Sutters joined for duty	JLM
"	11		In Trenches 2nd Lt R.B. Piper & 2nd Lt W.A Martin joined for duty	JLM
"	12		Relieved by 1/5th R War R HQ & 2 Companies Garrison of FONQUEVILLERS	JLM
"	13		In Support 2 Companies to LA HAIE	JLM
"	14		In Support	JLM
"	15		In Support 2nd Lt F.B. Williams joined for duty	JLM
"	16		In Support	JLM

FOWestmacott Lt Col.

Army Form C. 2118.

WAR DIARY
or
INTELLIGENCE SUMMARY.

1/6 R. War. Regt.   January 1916.

(Erase heading not required.)

Instructions regarding War Diaries and Intelligence Summaries are contained in F. S. Regs., Part II. and the Staff Manual respectively. Title pages will be prepared in manuscript.

Place	Date	Hour	Summary of Events and Information	Remarks and references to Appendices
FONQUEVILLERS	Jan 17		In Support	J.J.M.
	18		In Support	J.J.M.
	19		In Support	J.J.M.
	20		Relieved 1/5 R. War. R. in trenches – 1/4th Bat on right – 1/8th R. War. R. on left	J.J.M.
	21		1/5 Bat relieved 1/4th Bat	J.J.M.
	22		In Trenches. Casualties 1 O.R. wounded	J.J.M.
	23		In Trenches	J.J.M.
	24		In Trenches	J.J.M.
	25		In Trenches. Draft of 5 H.O's. Sector heavily shelled from 2 a.m. to 2.30 a.m.	J.J.M.
	26		In Trenches	J.J.M.
	27		In Trenches. 1/4th Bat relieved 1/5th Bat	J.J.M.
	28		Relieved by 1/5th R. War. Regt. Moved to Brigade Reserve at BAYENCOURT.	J.J.M.
BAYENCOURT	29		In Brigade Reserve	J.J.M.
	30		" Stood to 2.30 a.m. to 3.30 a.m. for proposed Raid	J.J.M.
	31		" Major H.E. Pitman handed over to 2/Lt R. Lane as 2nd in Command	J.J.M.

Army Form C. 2118.

1/6th R War R WAR DIARY Jan. 1916
or
INTELLIGENCE SUMMARY.

(Erase heading not required.)

Instructions regarding War Diaries and Intelligence Summaries are contained in F. S. Regs., Part II. and the Staff Manual respectively. Title pages will be prepared in manuscript.

Place	Date	Hour	Summary of Events and Information	Remarks and references to Appendices
FONQUEVILLERS	17		In Support	9th
"	18		In Support	9th
"	19		In Support	9th
"	20		Relieved 1/5th R War R in Trenches - 144th Bde on right - 1/8th R War R on left	9th
"	21		In Trenches 145th Bde relieved 144th Bde	9th
"	22		In Trenches Casualties 1 O R wounded	9th
"	23		In Trenches	9th
"	24		In Trenches	9th
"	25		In Trenches Draft of 54 O R - Sector heavily shelled from 2am to 2.00am	9th
"	26		In Trenches	9th
"	27		In Trenches 144th Bde relieved 145th Bde	9th
"	28		Relieved by 1/5th R War R. Moved to Brigade Reserve at BAYENCOURT	9th
BAYENCOURT	29		In Brigade Reserve	9th
"	30		"	9th
"	31		Stood to 2.30am to 3.20am for proposed Raid	9th

Townshend Lt Col.

143/48

1/6 R War Regt
Feb 1916.
Vol XII

Army Form C. 2118.

1/6th R War R WAR DIARY February 1916

INTELLIGENCE SUMMARY.

(Erase heading not required.)

Instructions regarding War Diaries and Intelligence Summaries are contained in F. S. Regs., Part II. and the Staff Manual respectively. Title pages will be prepared in manuscript.

Place	Date	Hour	Summary of Events and Information	Remarks and references to Appendices
BAYENCOURT	1/2		In Brigade Reserve	9 a.m.
"	2 Feb		In Brigade Reserve	9 a.m.
"	3		In Brigade Reserve	9 a.m.
"	4		In Brigade Reserve	9 a.m.
FONQUEVILLERS	5		Relieved 1/5th R War R in Trenches - 5th R War R on left - 4th Oxfords on right	9 a.m.
	6		In Trenches Casualties O.R. 1 Killed 1 Wounded (3rd Draft of 12 O.R.	9 p.m.
	7		In Trenches	9 a.m.
	8		In Trenches Capt A.D. WILCOX & Lieut H.L. FIELD joined for duty	9 a.m.
	9		In Trenches Casualties O.R. 2 Killed 4 Wounded	9 a.m.
	10		In Trenches	9 a.m.
	11		In Trenches Draft 5 O.R.	9 a.m.
	12		In Trenches	9 a.m.
	13		Relieved by 1/5th R War R H.Q. & 2 Companies to FONQUEVILLERS, & 2 Coo to LA HAIE	9 a.m.
	14		In Support Northern portion of FONQUEVILLERS taken over from 3 y 4 Div.	9 a.m.
	15		In Support	9 a.m.
	16		In Support Lt R C MARTIN joined for duty	9 a.m.

W.R. Dobbs Capt.
O.C. 1/6 R War R

Army Form C. 2118.

1/5 R.W.ar.R

WAR DIARY
February 1916
or
INTELLIGENCE SUMMARY.
(Erase heading not required.)

Instructions regarding War Diaries and Intelligence Summaries are contained in F. S. Regs., Part II. and the Staff Manual respectively. Title pages will be prepared in manuscript.

Place	Date	Hour	Summary of Events and Information	Remarks and references to Appendices
FONQUEVILLERS	17		In Support.	John.
"	18		In Support. Stood by 1-30 a.m. to 4 a.m. Raid on O Sector	J.L.M.
"	19		In Support	J.L.M
"	20		In Support	J.L.M
"	21		Relieved 1/5th R. War R in trenches. 1/5th R. War R on left. 4th Oxfords on right.	J.L.M
"	22		In Trenches	J.L.M
"	23		In Trenches	J.L.M
"	24		In Trenches	J.L.M
"	25		In Trenches	J.L.M
"	26		In Trenches	J.L.M
"	27		In Trenches	J.L.M
"	28		In Trenches	J.L.M
"	29		Relieved by 1/5th R. War R. Moved to Divisional 9 Brigade Reserve at BAYENCOURT.	J.L.M

W.D.Ponds? Capt
O.C. 1/5 R. War R

143.
48

1/6 R Warwick
 Regt

Vol. XIII

March 1916.

S E C R E T.

1/6th BATTALION ROYAL WARWICKSHIRE REGIMENT.

OPERATION ORDER NO. 26.

Copy No. 2

Reference Map,
1/40,000, 57 D.

(1) The following moves will take place on March 3rd 1916.

    1/6 R.War.R. Headquarters and 2 Coys. from BAYENCOURT to SOUASTRE.

    All first line transport, 143rd Infantry Brigade, from BAYENCOURT to SOUASTRE.

    Detachment of Brigade Machine Gun Company from BAYENCOURT to SOUASTRE.

Move to take place under the orders of the Officer Commanding 1/6 R.War.R.

(2) Troops will parade in the following order :-

    1/6 R.WAR.R. - Signallers, D and B.Coys., Headquarters, Transport.
    Detachment Brigade Machine Gun Company.
    1/7 R.WAR.R. - Transport and Stores.
    1/5 R.WAR.R. -   ditto.
    1/8 R.WAR.R. -   ditto.

The head of the column will pass cross-roads J.4.b.8.2. at 3-30 p.m.

(3) All Officers' Kits, mess boxes, and spare blankets, to be ready stacked outside billets for Transport by 2 p.m.

(4) Dinners should be not later than 12 o'clock.

(5) On arrival at SOUASTRE, Companies and all detachments must report to Headquarters, 1/6 R.War.R., when billets are taken over.

(6) Captain A.B.Turner will be in command of A. and C.Coys. remaining in BAYENCOURT.

A.Company will be BRIGADE RESERVE, C.Coy., DIVISIONAL RESERVE.

                                                          Captain.

3rd March 1916.   Acting Adjutant 1/6 R. WAR. REGT.

Issued at 10-30 a.m.

    Copy No. 1 File.
             2 War Diary.
             3 Q.M. & T.O., 1/5 R.War.R.
             4 Q.M. & T.O., 1/6 R.War.R.
             5 Q.M. & T.O., 1/7 R.War.R.
             6 Q.M. & T.O., 1/8 R.War.R.
             7 O.C., Brigade M.G.Company.
             8 O.C., "B" Coy, 1/6 R.War.R.
             9 O.C., "D" Coy. 1/6 R.War.R.
           10 Headquarters, 1/6 R.War.R.

Army Form C. 2118.

WAR DIARY
or
INTELLIGENCE SUMMARY.

1/5th R War R   March 1916

(Erase heading not required.)

Instructions regarding War Diaries and Intelligence Summaries are contained in F. S. Regs., Part II. and the Staff Manual respectively. Title pages will be prepared in manuscript.

Place	Date	Hour	Summary of Events and Information	Remarks and references to Appendices
BAYENCOURT	1/3		In Divisional and Brigade Reserve	J/M
"	2		Do	J/M
"	3		Do H.Q. & 2 Companies – all front line	J/M
			Transport of 143rd Inf. Bde moved to SOUASTRE – 2 Coo left at BAYENCOURT.	
SOUASTRE	4		In Divisional and Brigade Reserve	J/M
"	5		Do	J/M
"	6		Do	J/M
"	7		Do	J/M
FONCQUEVILLERS	8		Relieved 1/5th R.War.R. in Trenches 1 to 12. 1/8th R War R on left – 1/4th Oxfords on right	J/M
"	9		In Trenches	J/M
"	10		Do	J/M
"	11		Do Lt. K HERNE & 2/Lt H.E. CLARKE & 10 O.R. joined for duty	J/M
"	12		Do Reinforcement 2 O.R.	J/M
"	13		Do Casualties 1 O.R. wounded	J/M
"	14		Do 2 Further Lewis Guns received	J/M
"	15		Do making total number 6.	J/M

Army Form C. 2118.

1/6th R War R March 1916

WAR DIARY
or
INTELLIGENCE SUMMARY.
(Erase heading not required.)

Instructions regarding War Diaries and Intelligence Summaries are contained in F.S. Regs., Part II. and the Staff Manual respectively. Title pages will be prepared in manuscript.

Place	Date	Hour	Summary of Events and Information	Remarks and references to Appendices
FONQUEVILLERS	16		Relieved by 1/5th R War R. H.Q. & 2 Coys in garrison of FONQUEVILLERS — 2 Coys detached at LAHAIE, FORT DICK, JUNCTIONKEEP	J & M
"	17		Reinforcement 46 O.R. Casualties 1 O.R.	J & M
"	18		"	J & M
"	19		"	Corr S
"	20		"	Corr S
"	21		"	Corr S
"	22		"	Corr S
"	23		In early morning (12:50 AM.) Combined raid by 5th & 8th Batt on Huns trenches. 8th Batt entered trenches, & found without any dead, returned with 1 prisoner.	Corr S
"	24		Relieved 1/5 Rifles in trenches. 18 R.I.R. on Left, 11 Worc B on Right. H. 5 Officers & 20 NCOs & Men 18 Durham L.I. attached to us. Left on morning of 26th.	App S
"	25		"	2118
"	26		Trenches very quiet	Corr S
"	27		" 5 Officers & 20 O.R. 14th York & Lancs Regt attached until 31st	J & M
"	28		"	J & M
"	29		"	J & M
"	30		Reinforcement 1 O.R.	J & M
"	31		Casualties 1 O.R. wounded (Shell Shock)	J & M

[827] W 13345. 182 5000m 12/15s G & S 77 77
Forms C. 348 / 61

Army Form C. 348.

MEMORANDUM.

From Officer Commanding
1st Bn. R.War.Regt.

To Officer Commanding
6th Bn. R.War.Regt.

From O C /6th R War R

To A G: Office Base

ANSWER.

Field

8th March 1916.

Field.

11 March 1916.

The attached is passed to you, please, as it appears to have been addressed to this Battalion in error.

We are convinced that these must be the original copies — we are in possession of copies ours elves and feel confident they were not taken in duplicate.

G. H. Jacob Capt for Lieut-Col.
Comdg, 1st Bn. R.War.Regt.

J. Miller Capt /Adj
6th R War R

CENTRAL REGISTRY
14 MAR 1916
C.R. No. 8700/275.

Subject:- Duplicate War Diaries.

To:-

A.G.'s OFFICE AT THE BASE
CENTRAL REGISTRY
-3 MAR 1916
C.R. No. 8700/275

CONFIDENTIAL

1st R. Warwick Regt

The enclosed Duplicate War Diary is returned to you please, as "Duplicates" are not required in this Office, vide:- General Routine Order, No. 1125.

A J Kennington L
for Major.,
for D. A. G.,

G.H.Q.,
3rd Echelon,
2/3/1916.

143/48

1/6 R Warwick Regt

Vol XIII

April 1916.

SECRET.   Copy No.....2....

1/6TH BATTALION THE ROYAL WARWICKSHIRE REGIMENT.

OPERATION ORDER NO. 27.

Reference Map,
Sheet 57D. 1/40,000.

1. The garrison of FONQUEVILLERS will be withdrawn on the 26th instant.

2. Headquarters and two Companies will move to billets at SOUASTRE, and two Companies will remain at LA HAIE.

3. Garrisons of FORT DICK and JUNCTION KEEP will be relieved by the 5th ROYAL SUSSEX REGT., at 10 a.m.

4. (a) On relief these garrisons will move by half platoons along VALLEY trench via Western side of LA HAIE to SOUASTRE.

   (b) D. and A. Companies, less 1½ platoons, will move via CEMETERY ROAD as far as metalled, and then along valley to FONQUEVILLERS-SOUASTRE Road, leaving by half platoons at 200 yards interval - first party of D.Coy. passing the BRASSERIE at 9 a.m.

5. Advance party of 2/Lieut. C.T.Morris-Davies for Headquarters, and one subaltern from each Company, will reach SOUASTRE by 9.30 a.m. to hand over billets to their respective Coys.

6. Cookers will be ready to move at 8 a.m.

7. Officers kits' and mess boxes, also Pioneers, Signallers, and Orderly Room baggage, will be ready by 9 a.m.

8. Lewis Gun transport, mess cart, and maltese cart, will report at 9.30 a.m.

9. Not more than two men to proceed with any vehicle : remainder to proceed by the above mentioned route.

                              (Signed)   J. L. MELLOR, Captain.

Issued at 2.30 p.m.   ADJUTANT 1/6TH BATT. R. WAR. R.
April 25th 1916.

        Copy No. 1.   File.
                 2.   War Diary.
                 3.   O.C., "A" Coy.
                 4.   O.C., "B" Coy.
                 5.   O.C., "C" Coy.
                 6.   O.C., "D" Coy.
                 7.   Headquarters.
                 8.   O.C., LA HAIE Detachment.
                 9.   Transport Officer.
                 10.   Quartermaster.
                 11.   Sergeant Major.

Army Form C. 2118.

WAR DIARY
or
INTELLIGENCE SUMMARY.

1/6th R War R   April 1916

(Erase heading not required.)

Instructions regarding War Diaries and Intelligence Summaries are contained in F. S. Regs., Part II. and the Staff Manual respectively. Title pages will be prepared in manuscript.

Place	Date	Hour	Summary of Events and Information	Remarks and references to Appendices
SOUASTRE	1/4/16		Relieved by 1/5th R War R. Moved to SOUASTRE in Brigade's Divisional Reserve	J d h
"	2nd		A patrol sent out in early morning to reconnoitre enemy's sap - 2nd Lt. R B Piper wounded and missing - Casualties 1 O R seriously wounded.	J d h
"	3rd		In Reserve. 2nd Lt. B. G. SUTHERS returned to England	J d h
"	4th		" 2nd Lt. A. R. DOWNING joined for duty on 4th	J d h
"	5th		"	J d h
"	6th		"	J d h
"	7th		"	J d h
"	8th		" 2nd Lt. Price rejoined from Base	J d h
FONQUEVILLERS	9th		Relieved 1/5th R War R in trenches. 1/5th R War R on left - Bucks R on right	J d h
"	10		In Trenches. 2 Officers of 16th West Yorks attached for 48 hours	J d h
"	11		"	J d h
"	12		"	J d h
"	13		" 1 Off 16th West Yorks & 1 Off 15th West Yorks attached for 48 hours	J d h
"	14		" Casualties 1 O R wounded	J d h
"	15		" Reinforcement 10 O R. Major W H FRANKLIN 1/1 Newfoundland Regt taken over command	J d h
"	16		" 3 Off 18th Durham Light Infantry attached for 48 hours	J d h

W H Franklin A/Col.

1577 Wt. W10791/1773 500,000 1/15 D. D. & L. A.D.S.S./Forms/C. 2118.

Army Form C. 2118.

1/6th R War R   April 1916

WAR DIARY
or
INTELLIGENCE SUMMARY.
(Erase heading not required.)

Instructions regarding War Diaries and Intelligence
Summaries are contained in F. S. Regs., Part II
and the Staff Manual respectively. Title pages
will be prepared in manuscript.

Place	Date	Hour	Summary of Events and Information	Remarks and references to Appendices
FONQUEVILLERS	17		Relieved by 1/5th R War R. H.Q. & 2 Coys garrison of FONQUEVILLERS. 2 Coys form Detachment at LA HAIE	9thm
	18		In Support	9thm
	19			9thm
	20			9thm
	21			9thm
	22			9thm
	23		Casualties 1 O.R. wounded.	9thm
	24		" " " "	9thm
	25		" " " "	9thm
SOUASTRE	26		In Divisional Reserve. Evacuated FONQUEVILLERS - H.Q. & 2 Coys moved to billets at SOUASTRE. 2 Coys billeted at LA HAIE	9thm
	27		Training	9thm
	28		"	9thm
	29		2 O.R. 2 Companies called up to R. Sectn and placed under command of 144th Brigade - Casualties 4 O.R. seriously wounded	9thm
	30		Above companies returned 6.30 a.m.	

Will H Franklin Lt Col

D. A. G.,
   3rd Echelon.
   _____

   Enclosed please find Battalion War Diary for
the month of May 1916.

                               [signature]
                                         Lieut-Col.,
2/6/1916.   Commanding 1/6th Bn. R. War. Regt.

1/6th R War R
May 1916

WAR DIARY or INTELLIGENCE SUMMARY

Army Form C. 2118.

Place	Date	Hour	Summary of Events and Information	Remarks and references to Appendices
SOUASTRE	1		In Divisional Reserve. Lieut R.C. LOWE required 34 O.R. joined	J & M
	2		Moved to L Section and relieved 1/5th Worcester Regt. at 3.30 p.m. 1/6th R War on left. Bucks Batt on right.	J & M
FONQUEVILLERS	2		In Trenches	J & M
"	3	"		J & M
"	4	"		J & M
"	5	"	Relieved by 1/5th S. Staffs Regt. Moved to Bivouac at COUIN in Divisional Reserve	J & M
COUIN	6	"	In Divisional Reserve.	J & M
"	7	"		J & M
"	8	"	Moved to Bivouac at COURCELLES for digging. 2nd/Lt S.J. WINKLEY joined	J & M
COURCELLES	9	"		J & M
"	10	"	Moved to Bivouac at AUTHIE. 2/Lts. W.P. WHEELER, R.V. ROSE and H.R. BUTTERY joined.	J & M
AUTHIE				J & M
GEZAINCOURT	11	"	Marched with whole Brigade to billets at GEZAINCOURT.	J & M
"	12	"		J & M
"	13	"	Reinforcement 31. O.R.	J & M
"	14	"		J & M
"	15	"	Reinforcement 28. O.R.	J & M
"	16	"		J & M
"	17	"		J & M

W.H. Ironmonger
Lt Col
1/6 R War R

Army Form C. 2118.

1/8th R.W.Sa.R   May 1918

WAR DIARY
or
INTELLIGENCE SUMMARY.

(Erase heading not required.)

Instructions regarding War Diaries and Intelligence Summaries are contained in F. S. Regs., Part II. and the Staff Manual respectively. Title pages will be prepared in manuscript.

Place	Date	Hour	Summary of Events and Information	Remarks and references to Appendices
GEZAINCOURT	18		In Divisional Reserve	J.d.M.
"	19			J.d.M.
"	20			J.d.M.
"	21		Reinforcement 1 O.R.	J.d.M.
"	22		Stokes Gun Accident Casualties 2 O.R. Killed & 2 O.R. Wounded	J.d.M.
"	23			J.d.M.
COUIN	24		Marched to Couin with Brigade. Attacked over country BOISNEUX to COUIN on 25th Brigade Practice	(24)-8
"	25			(24)-8
"	26		Attacks proceeded with from COUIN & AUTHIE.	(24)-8
AUTHIE	27		Returned from Authie	(24)-8
GAZAINCOURT	28		In Divisional Reserve	(2M)S
"	29		In Divisional Reserve	(2M)S
"	30		"	24F
COUIN	31		Brigade marched to COUIN to bivouac	(24)S

Willi Frankin
Lt Col
1/8 RWSaR

1577 Wt. W10791/1773 500,000 1/15 D. D. & L.   A.D.S.S./Forms/C. 2118.

SECRET.   Copy No...1......

1/6TH BATTALION THE ROYAL WARWICKSHIRE REGIMENT.

OPERATION ORDER No.28.

Ref.Map.
57D.1/40,000.   1st May, 1916.

1. 1/6th R.WAR.R. will relieve 1/8th WORCESTER REGT. on the afternoon of May 1st., commencing at 3.30 p.m.

2. Dispositions of Companies will be :-

   "B" Coy. on the RIGHT.
   "D" "   "   " LEFT.
   "C" "   will find INLYING PICQUET & SUPPORT.
   "A" "   will be in reserve.

3. Companies from the CHATEAU will move under orders of Major Deakin, "C" Coy. following "B".

4. "D" Coy's first half platoon will move at 2.15 p.m. via DUMMY GUN and CEMETERY ROAD Route, followed at 200 yards interval by the remaining platoons of "D" and "A" Coys.

   Headquarters details and all details of Companies will parade outside Battalion Headquarters at 3 p.m.

5. Horses for cookers will report to the various Companies at 1-30 pm

6. Limbers for officers' kits and Lewis Guns & magazines will report at LA HAIE at 1-30 p.m., also at "A" and "D" Coys at 1-30 p.m. They will collect all spare kit for return to the Q.M. as they come back from the trenches, one man being left in charge in each case.

7. Officers' mess cart and maltese cart will report at Battalion Headquarters at 2.15 p.m.

8. Particular care will be taken in taking over all trench stores and returns made to the Adjutant.

9. Company officers must reduce all mess stuff to the minimum as a move is anticipated direct from the trenches.

10. The Commanding Officer will see all O.C.Coys at Battalion Headquarters at 6 p.m.

                                            J L Mellor
                                            Captain.
Issued at   m.   Adjutant 1/6 Batt.R.WAR.R.
1st May,1916.

       Copy No. 1   War Diary.
                2   File.
                3   O.C., "A" Coy.
                4   O.C., "B" "
                5   O.C., "C" "
                6   O.C., "D" "
                7   O.C., LA HAIE Detachment.
                8   Headquarters.
                9   Transport Officer.
               10   Sergeant Major.

SECRET.   Copy No... 2

OPERATION ORDERS NO. 29.

by

LIEUT COLONEL W.H.FRANKLIN COMMANDING 1/6TH BATTALION
THE ROYAL WARWICKSHIRE REGIMENT.

Reference Map,
57 D 1/40,000.

1. The 1/6th Battalion The Royal Warwickshire Regiment will be relieved by the 5th Battalion South Staffordshire Regiment on May 5th, commencing at 3 p.m., when the Battalion will march to billets at COUIN.

2. One officer per Company and one N.C.O. per platoon, who possess a good knowledge of the line, are to be attached to the relieving Companies holding the front trenches for a period of 24 hours after relief.

3. O.C.Coys. will detail one guide per platoon to be at CROSS ROADS D.22.d.8.3. at 2-15 p.m. to conduct platoons of the 5th South Staffs. to the trenches via the DUMMY GUN Route.

   "A" Coy. will guide platoons of "B" Coy., South Staffs.Regt.
   "B" "   "   "   "   " "A" "   "   "   "
   "C" "   "   "   "   " "D" "   "   "   "
   "D" "   "   "   "   " "C" "   "   "   "

4. In addition, the two Companies in the line will detail a guide for the garrison of each post.   They should be at the POLICE BARRIER at 2-45 p.m.

5. The route for relief is as follows:- CEMETERY ROAD & DUMMY GUN Route, moving by half platoons at 200 yards distance as far as D.23.c.7.5., where each Company will assemble and march to billets at COUIN.

6. 2/Lieut.C.T.Morris-Davies, Company Q.M.Sergeants, and one junior N.C.O. from each platoon, will rendezvous at Battalion Headquarters at 12-30 p.m. and proceed to COUIN to take over billets.
   They should then meet the incoming troops at junction of roads D.25.c.9.9. at about 5 p.m.

7. Cookers will move at 1-30 p.m., tea being ready for troops on arrival.

8. All vehicles must move singly at a distance of 200 yards.

9. All trench stores shewn on lists issued to Companies, together with all maps of FONQUEVILLERS 1/10,000, will be handed over with an inventory and a receipt obtained in duplicate, one of which will be handed to the Adjutant immediately on relief.

   All other stores will be taken out on relief.

10. All blankets are to be rolled in tens, numbered, and stacked near ARTILLERY X ROADS by 1 p.m., one man per Company being left in charge.

11. All excess Lewis Gun magazines must be outside Pioneer Sergeant's store in village by 1 p.m., guns and magazines in posts being taken out as soon as relieved.

12. Officers' baggage and mess boxes are to be stacked outside Pioneer Sergt's store by 1-30 p.m.

13. Separate orders are being issued to Transport Officer.

J L Mellor
Captain.

Issued at   p.m.

Adjutant 1/6th Battalion The Royal Warwickshire Regiment.

4th May, 1916.

```
Copy No.  1      File.
          2      War Diary.
          3      O.C., A. Coy.
          4      O.C., B.  "
          5      O.C., C.  "
          6      O.C., D.  "
          7      Headquarters.
          8      Transport Officer.
          9      Quartermaster.
         10      Sergeant Major.
```

SECRET.

1/6th Bn. ROYAL WARWICKSHIRE REGT.   Copy No 2

Map Reference 57.D.N.E.1/20,000   <u>Operation Order No.31.</u>

1. The Battalion will move into bivouacs at J.16 D. to-morrow

2. Battalion will fall in on Battalion Alarm Post, ready to move off, at 11.20 a.m., moving in the following order:- H.Q., A., B., C., D..

3. One N.C.O. from each company and H.HQ. will report to Lieut. Morgan at 8.30 a.m. to proceed to take over bivouacs from 6th Gloucesters.

4. Lieut. K. Brown will arrange transport of Lewis Guns and magazines.

5. 1 G. S. Wagon and 4 Limbers will call for Officers' kits and Mess Boxes at 10.30 a.m.

6. Officers' horses will be ready at 11.15 a.m.

7. Company Cookers will be ready at 11 o'clock.

                                             2/Lieut. & A/Adjt.,
31st May 1916.   for O/C 1/6th R. War. R.

        Copy No.1 File   Copy No.7. Headquarters
             2 War Diary   8 Transport Officer
             3 A Coy.   9 Quartermaster
             4 B "   10 Sergt.Major.
             5 C "
             6 D "

SECRET.　　　　　　　　　　　　　　　　　　　　　　　COPY NO. 2

1/6th Battalion ROYAL WARWICKSHIRE REGIMENT.

OPERATION ORDER NO. 30

Reference
Map 57 D.1/40,000

1. The Battalion will move, as part of the Brigade, into bivouacs at COUIN on 25th inst.

2. The head of the Battalion will be at bridge, A.27.c.5.4. facing south, ready to move at 3.5 a.m., and will move in the following order:- SIGNALLERS, C, D, A, B,

3. B Company will detail 12 brakesmen to report to Transport Officer at 3 a.m., also 1 Officer and 6 men to march in rear of the whole Brigade column from the starting point, A.22.b.7.8.

4. The Brigade is to take part in a tactical exercise on the 26th inst., bivouac at AUTHIE that night and return to present billets on the 27th instant.

5. A halt will be made for breakfast about 6 a.m.

6. All stores, officers' valises, and mess boxes, not required, are to be stacked near the Orchard or by Q.M's Stores, at which places guards will be posted during the absence of the Battalion.

7. In addition to mess boxes one package or valise per company for officers' kits will be allowed.

Mess Cart and Limber for these packages will be at Headquarters at 2.40 a.m. Outside Orchard billet at 3.50 a.m.

Issued at 3.15 p.m.　　　　　　　　　　　　　　　Captain.
24th May 1916.　　　　Adjutant 1/6th Batt. Royal Warwickshire Regt.

```
Copy No. 1    File
         2    War Diary.
         3    O/C., A Coy.
         4    O/C   B   "
         5    O/C   C   "
         6    O/C   D   "
         7    Headquarters
         8    Transport Officer
         9    Quartermaster
        10    Sergeant Major.
```

Army Form C. 2118.

WAR DIARY
or
INTELLIGENCE SUMMARY.

(Erase heading not required.)

1/6 R Warwick Regt for June 1916

Vol 16

Place	Date	Hour	Summary of Events and Information	Remarks and references to Appendices
N. SAILLY	June 1		Marched to bivouac near Sailly went into Brigade reserve.	(2M-8)
"	2		Brigade reserve.	(2M-8)
"	3		"	(2M-8)
"	4		" and a Patrol Carried in conjunction with Aeroplane.	(1M-8)
"	5		"	(1M-8)
"	6		" Battalion together with 5th Battn & 50 men from 8th Battn dug 6 deep out in)	(2M-8)
"	7		front of H Sector. Running out 120 yds & also put out a belt of wire 4 ft aut. & 800 yds long the	(2M-8)
			whole by dawn. Casualties OR killed 1 missing 3 wounded. Worked 9-30PM – 1-45 AM on 7th.	(2M-8)
TRENCHES	8		Took over H sector relieved 5th Battalion in trenches. Worked on above scheme. 1 OR wounded	(2M-8)
"	9		continued above work all night	(3M-8)
"	10		Honours Lt. Col. F. O. Wetland C.M.G. Lieut L.L Greeman M.C. & Lieut P.M Radmore M.C.	(2M-8)
"	11			Casualties 1 OR killed 2 wounded 3/2M8
"	12			(2M-8)
"	13		Relieved by 5th 6 Cheshires marched to Bresnon.	(2M-8)
BEAUVAL	14		Marched with 8th Battn to Beauval, since attached to 11 Brigade	(2M-8)
"	15		Training continued	(2M-8)
"	16		"	(2M-8)
"	17		"	(2M-8)
"	18		"	
"	19			Lieut J N Stafford Regimen Battn as reinforcement.
"	20			Reinforcements 16 OR
				3 OR

Army Form C. 2118.

WAR DIARY
or
INTELLIGENCE SUMMARY.

1/6th R War R   June 1916

(Erase heading not required.)

Place	Date	Hour	Summary of Events and Information	Remarks and references to Appendices
BEAUVAL	21st		In Reserve for Training Reinforcement 4 O R	J.M.
"	22		" " " 1 O R	J.M.
VAUCHELLES	23		Moved to billets at VAUCHELLES.	J.M.
"	24		Training & Equipping	J.M.
BEAUSSART	25		Moved to billets at BEAUSSART	J.M.
MAILLY MAILLET	26		HdQrs & 2 Companies moved to MAILLY MAILLET billets – 2 Cos took over sector of line SERRE Road exclusive to Trench 35/4 inclusive – On Stairs, 1st line transport to BERTRANCOURT. Casualties 1 O.R. killed 1 O.R. Wounded	J.M.
"	27		In MAILLY. Reinforcement 30 O.R. Six Platoons employed in clearing front line – enemy fired very heavy barrage flattening the front line system of trenches. Casualties O.R. 5 killed, Missing 16 Wounded & 2/2d R Battery wounded (Proposed raid abandoned)	J.M.
"	28		In MAILLY & trenches Casualties O.R. 5 Wounded	J.M.
"	29		In MAILLY Two Companies relieved from trenches by 8th R War R Reinforcement 6 O R	J.2.M.
"	30		In MAILLY Marched to Assembly Trenches at 10.30 p.m. Number for Roll call 24 Officers 626 O R	J.M.

J.J. Mallaby Capt
O.C. 1/6th R War R

SECRET.   21st June, 1916.   1.   COPY No. 2
                                                                34
                                        OPERATION ORDER NO.........
        OPERATION ORDERS BY LIEUT. COL. W.H. FRANKLIN COMMANDING
                   1/6th ROYAL WARWICKSHIRE REGtT.

        Reference   Map 1/20,000   57D N.E. & S.E.
                      " 1/10,000   Trench Map Hebuterne & Beaumont.

1. The Battalion is to take part attached to the 11th. Brigade in
    an assault on a day to be called Z. The time of the assault
    will be Zero.

2. BOMBARDMENT.   The preliminary bombardment will cover a period
                    of five days to be known as U V W X Y.

3. Gas & SMOKE.   If wind favourable Gas and Smoke will be used
                    during the artillery bombardment.

4. Preliminary Move. On W X night "D" & "C" Coys. will take
                       over protion of trenches on the left of the
    line now held by the 10th. Inf. Brigade. from SERRE ROAD exclusive
    to K 35 No. 4 Trench inclusive. Batalion H.Qrs. will be
    at LYCEUM.   "B" & "A" Coys will be billetted in MAILLY MAILLET.

                On Y Z "A" & "B" coys. will take up positions
    of assembly in accordance with attached table.   All units of
    the Brigade must have passed the line of AUCHONVILLERS & EUSTON
    (K 33 A) ROAD by 12 midnight.   All units of the Brigade must
    be in their assembly trenches by 1-30 a.m. on Z day.   At least
    1 Officer & NCO per platoon are to reconnoitre both by day and
    night the route allotted to the Battalion.   No smoking or light
    will be permitted after battalions have paraded to march off
    from their billets.   The strictest silence is to be observed
    during the march.   All ranks will be warned to take the
    greatest care not to disclose to the enemy the fact that our
    positions of assembly have been occupied.

5. PREPARING WIRE. The Coys. holding the line will be
                     responsible for cutting the wire in front of
    our front lines and as far back as the line VALLADE-CHEAPSIDE
    inclusive.   Lanes will be cut diagonally in all wire and this
    will be carried out during X/Y and Y/Z nights.
                The Coys. in occupation of the line during
    the preliminary bombardment will be responsible for keeping
    gaps in the enemy wire by bursts of Rifle and Machine Gun Fire.
                The artillery will cut the whole of the
    wire on the enemy front line - the wire Q 5 a 8.1 - Q 5 a 4.0 -
    and will make a 5 yard path every 20 yards in all other wire.
                During the preliminary bombardments Lieuts.
    A.W.Chovil and H.R.Buttery will be present at the O.P. of wire
    cutting batteries.   Positions of these posts will be notified.
                These two officers will reconnoitre the
    enemy's wire by night and report on the results of the artillery
    fire.   For this purpose there will be no artillery fire
    on the enemy's front line between the hours named below:-
                2nd. night   11 p.m.   to   midnight.
                3rd.   "   10-30 p.m.   "   11-30 p.m.
                4th.   "   12 midnight   "   1-0 a.m.
                5th.   "   11-30 p.m.   "   12-30 a.m.

SECRET.   21st June, 1916.   2.   COPY No.........contd.

OPERATION ORDER NO. 34.

6. ARTILLERY LIFTS.   The artillery will lift off the German front line at Zero hour, at which hour the Infantry will assault. Subsequent lifts will be as follows:-
Off objective:-
1/ Hants.   )
1/ Somerset Light Infy.))   0.45 hours.
6th R. Warwicks. Regt.   )

Heavy Artillery will lift in all cases 5 minutes beforehand. At the commencement of each Infantry attack Divisional Artillery will lift 100 yards and will continue lifting at the rate of 50 yards per minute to the objective, firing 3 rounds of gun fire at each step.   The heavy artillery will lift straight on to objective. Infantry must noth arrive at the successive objectives before the time given of artillery lifts but must make their pace conform to the artillery lifts.

If the infantry are checked by our own barrage they must halt and wait until the barrage moves forward.

7. CONTACT AEROPLANE PATROLS.   During the attack 2 aeroplanes will be employed as contact patrols on the Corps Front. These aeroplanes will pick up the position of Brigade and Battn. Hd. Qrs. and the position of the front line and will also receive signals from the above Hd. Qrs. For this purpose Bde. and Batt. Hd. Qrs. will take forward one ground sheet for signalling to aeroplane and four flares will be carried by each Officer and N.C.O.

8. ATTACK.   At Zero hour the leading wave of the 8th R.War.R. must be formed up in No Man s Land parallel to the objective. The 8th R. War.R. will detail special parties to bomb down trenches leading to K 29 d 6.1. and Point 18, to join hands with the 31st Division.

The Battalion is the left battalion of the second line of the 11th Bde. The others being 1/ Somerset Light Infy. on our right with the 1/Hants on their right. These battalions will advance at 0.10 hours. Each battalion will have two coys. in the front line and two in support. Each Coy. will be on a frontage of two Platoons. Companies will, as far as possible, move in columns of sections, moving to a flank in file at 30 paces interval between sections and 100 yards distance between waves.

9. DIVIDING LINES. Between 1/Somerset Light Infy. and 6th R.War.R. K 35 d 4.9   K 36 c 3.2   all inclusive to 1/Somerset Light Infy.

Between 6th R.War.R. and 31st Division K 36 a 0.5   K 36 a 6.3. communication trench joining these points inclusive to 6th R.War.R.

10. ACTION on REACHING OBJECTIVE.   Consolidate the position.

Special party under 2/Lieut. Balkwill to construct strong point at Point 63. Special party under 2/Lt. Field to construct a strong point at Point 28. The latter will be assisted by party from C Coy. under 2/Lt. Buttery. A party from D Coy. under Cpl. Stevens will assist 2/Lt. Balkwill. Covering parties as already detailed, will at once take up their positions. Companies to re-organize at earliest opportunity.

SECRET.   21st June, 1916.   2.   COPY.................

OPERATION   ORDER No. 34.

OPERATION ORDERS BY LIEUT.COL. W.H. FRANKLIN COMMANDING
1/6th ROYAL WARWICKSHIRE REGT.

    Reference:-   Map 1/20,000   .57 D N.E. & S.E.
                             "   1/10,000   Trench Map

SECRET.   21st June, 1916.   3.   COPY NO............
                                        34
                               OPERATION ORDER NO......contd.

11.   FURTHER ACTION.   At 1-30 hours special patrols from 1/Hants, 1/Somerset Light Infy. & 6th R.War.R. will move forward to cut wire running N. & S. between BEAUCOURT SERRE & PUISIEUX ROAD. None of our artillery fire will be west of this line after 1-35 hours.
      Patrol from 1/6th R.War.R. will be sent forward at the same hour to the trench running northward from Point 45 towards PENDANT COPSE to gain touch with the 31st Div.
      (Further details will be issued concerning these parties).

12.   PATROLS.   6th R.War.R. will detail special parties to bomb down trench leading to Point 79 also to trench running down to 10 TREE ALLEY.

13.   TRAFFIC in COMMUNICATION TRENCHES.   From 2 a.m. Saturday, Communication Trenches are allotted as follows:-
      All up traffic will proceed by the following routes:-
         Cheerho Avenue   - Wolf Street.
            "   "   - Burrow Trench.
         Newgate Street
         (if completed)   - Delauney Avenue.

      All down traffic by one or other of the following routes
         Egg Street   - Vallade Corner-6th Avenue
         Borden Avenue   - 6th Avenue.

14.   MEDICAL ARRANGEMENTS.   Collecting posts will be established at Near Hyde Park Corner off ROMAN ROAD, K 34 c 3.9. Cellar at Cross Road 33 c 2.6.
      The Junction of Borden Avenue & Fox Street with front line trench will be marked by a red & white chequered flag to denote the points at which Stretcher Bearers will enter evacuation trenches. These flags will be placed in position by the 12th Field Ambulance.

15.   BATTALION HEADQUARTERS.   Battalion Headquarters runners & signallers etc. will move with the 4th wave and re-establish themselves at Point 81 remaining there until they can move up to Point 28 in the final objective. All messages to be sent to these centres.

16.   PRISONERS of WAR.   The 12th Bde. will hand over prisoners to 6th R. War. R. at or near Point 63. These & any taken by the battalion will be escorted to Brigade Collecting Station at VALLADE TRENCH.

17.   R.E. STORES.   The Battalion will carry forward material which will be dropped by them in the Final Objective Trench of the 8th R. War.R.   As soon as our Final Objective has been gained, battalion in rear will organize parties to carry forward this material to axxxxxxxxx dump which will be formed where communication trench S. of 10 TREE ALLEY joins our Final Objective.

18.   GRENADES.   on reaching final objective all men not going further forward on special parties and who are S. of Point 28 will pass up their grenades to a dump that will be formed at this point. Similarly, all men not going forward and who are N. of Point 28 and S. of Point 63 will pass up all grenades to R.E. DUMP referred to in section 17. This dump will be marked by a Blue & Yellow Flag and will be under the command of 2/Lt. Rose. Reserves are at MINOR STREET and in VALLADE TRENCH, these will be carried up by Brigade Carrying parties.

SECRET.   June 21st*16.   4   COPY NO.............

OPERATION ORDER NO' 34
              contd.

18. **GRENADES (contd).** In addition to the two grenades to be carried by every Officer, N.C.O. & man during the two day preparation of trench, 6 men from each Platoon will have issued to them 13 grenades in a Canvas Bucket.

19. **LEWIS GUNS.** Two extra carriers should be allotted to each team (making 8 men per team). Twelve buckets will be issued to each team,—in each of which 6 magazines will be carried,—as far as possible.

20. **S. A. A..** S.A.A. for Lewis Guns and Rifles will be brought up to dump by Brigade Carrying parties.

21. **FOOD.** Brigade Dump will be in VALLADE TRENCH. Coy. officers are responsible that 1 N.C.O. and 3 men are detailed to act as guides and shall report to the rendez-vous given by the Staff Capt OR to VALLADE TRENCH. This dump will be marked by signboard in Brigade Colours bearing Number of Brigade and at night with green lanterns. Ammunition dump will be marked by green & red lamps in pairs. Rations will be packed in twelves in 2 sandbags, these bags will be tied together. Two men will carry rations for 12 and water for 8.

22. **EQUIPMENT.** Pack & Great Coat will not be carried. Arrangements will be made for storing them in billets. If "C" & "D" Coys. take packs to trenches they will have to return them to MAILLY MAILLET on Y day. Every man will carry rifle and equipment less pack.

Haversack on back, Water Bottle on belt in centre of back. Entrenching Tool will be worn on right side, Ground Sheet tightly rolled in valise straps under haversack.
One bandolier S.A.A. making total 170 rounds.
    2 Mills Grenades No.5.   One Iron Ration (in Haversack)
    Two Sandbags.   One day Ration
    Two Smoke Helmets.   (complete)   "   "
    Mess Tin.

In addition every infantryman except Lewis Gunners and Bombers will carry a pick or shovel on back beneath equipment braces.

Bombers will not carry the additional bandolier.

Runners after reaching objective will remove their equipment and only carry rifle and bandolier.

Selected men carry wire cutters which have distinguishing strip of yellow cloth on lanyard, care must be taken to always remove wire cutters from casualties.

One man per Platoon throughout the Division will carry an Infantry Marking Fan.

Every Officer and N.C.O. will carry 4 flares, some will carry Very Lights and Pistols, details later.

23. **MAPS.** Only those maps referred to at head of orders are to be used in messages or orders or are to be carried in the attack. No map shewing our trenches will be taken. Officers and N.C.O. will carry note book. Nom private books or papers are to be carried.

SECRET.   21st June, 1916.   COPY NO..........

                        OPERATION ORDER NO...34   contd.

24   SYNCHRONISING of WATCHES.   Lieut. K. Brown will report
      at Brigade Hd. Qrs. at 1-45 p.m. on the afternoon of
      Y day.

25   Separate orders are being issued to T.O. Signals and
      Officer of Brigade Carrying Party.

                    (Signed) J.L. Mellor
                         Capt. & Adjt.
                    for O/C 1/6th R. Warwicks. Regt.

OPERATION ORDER NO. 35 ISSUED BY LIEUT. COL. W.H. FRANKLIN
COMMANDING 1/6th R. WARWICKSHIRE REGT.

COPY NO. 2

JUNE 22nd 1916.

Reference: Map,   LENS   Sheet 11.

1. Battalion will move to-morrow with 8th Battn. R. War.R. together with 11th Bde. Machine Gun Coy. and Trench Mortar Btty., 6th Battn. leading.
2. Battalion will march in following order:- Signallers, "C" "D" "A" and "B" Coys.
3. Transport will march at head of Bde. Transport behind Trench Mortar Bttys.
4. Head of the Column will pass Battn Hd. Qrs. in a Southerly direction at 7-40 a.m.
5. Horses will report for Cookers at 7-0 a.m.
6. All Officers' Kits, Mess Boxes, Q.M. Stores, Pioneers', Shoemaker and Orderly Room Boxes etc. will be outside Billets on the pathway by 6-25 a.m. These will be collected, starting from "B" Coy. and working uphill, at 6-30 a.m.
7. "B" Coy. will detail 20 men and 1 Officer to parade at Battn. Hd. Qrs. in full marching order at 6-30 a.m. These will there pile arms and leave their kits and act as Brakesmen for the Transport, the remainder marching in rear of the Battn.
8. Coy. Officers will hand to Adjt. at head of the Battn. by 7-35 a.m. numbers on parade stating Officers, N.C.O.'s and privates, also a certificate that all Billets occupied by them have been left in a clean condition.
9. Officers' horses will be ordered independently.
10. All details other than Signallers will march with Coys. only detailed Brakesmen being with Transport.

(Signed) J.L. MELLOR,
CAPT. & ADJT.
for O/C 1/6th R. Warwicks. Regt.

Copy No. 1   To File.
"   "   2   War Diary.
"   "   3   To "A" Coy.
"   "   4   " "B" "
"   "   5   " "C" "
"   "   6   " "D" "
"   "   7   " Transport Officer & Q.M.
"   "   8   " 8th Battn. R. Warwicks. Regt.
"   "   9   " Orderly Room.

Unit.	Route.	Starting Point.	Hd. of Bn. to pass S.P at.	Battn to be clear of S.P. by.
8/ Royal Fusiliers	By main road to SUCRERIE and thence to assembly trenches.	Railway crossing on MAILLY-MAILLET-SUCRERIE ROAD	10 pm.	10.20 pm.
1/ Rifle Brigade	ditto.	ditto.	10.20 "	10.40 "
6th Royal Warwicks (less Coys in trenches)	ditto.	ditto.	10.40 pm.	10.55 pm.

OPERATION ORDER NO. 36 ISSUED BY LIEUT. COL. W.H. FRANKLIN
COMMANDING 1/6th ROYAL WARWICKSHIRE REGIMENT.

June 25th, 1916.

Reference:- Map LENS Sheet 11.

1. Battalion will move to BEAUSSART this evening via LOUVENCOURT & BERTRANCOURT.

2. Battalion will march in the following order:- Signallers, "D", "A", "B" and "C" Coys. Transport will march immediately in rear of Battn.

3. Head of Column will be at Battn. Hd. Qrs. facing North and clear of the main MARIEUX - LOUVENCOURT Road at 9-40 p.m.

4. Horses will report for cookers at 9-0 p.m.

5. Mess Boxes must be reduced to a minimum and will be carried in crates by Coy. Cookers.

6. All Officers' Kits, Q.M. Stores, Pioneers, Shoemakers, & Orderly Room Boxes must be outside Billets by 8-45 p.m.

7. Officers' Kits will be collected by first wagon working up towards Headquarters.

8. "C" Coy. will detail 20 men and 1 Officer to report to Battn. Hd. Qrs. at 8-3p.m. in full marching order. They will pile arms and leave kits. After loading Transport commencing at Officers' Orchard, they will act as Brakesmen for Transport, the remainder marching in rear of the Battn.

9. Coy. Officers will hand to Adjt. at head of the Battn. by 9-30 p.m. numbers on parade stating Officers, N.C.O's and privates, also a certificate that all Billets occupied by them have been left in a clean condition.

10. Officers' Horses will be ordered independantly.

11. All Details other than Signallers will march with Coys. only detailed Brakesmen being with Transport.

(Signed) J.L. MELLOR, Capt. & Adjt.
for O/C 1/6th R. Warwicks. Regt.

Copy No. 1   To File.
        2   War Diary.
        3   To "A" Coy.
        4   "B" "
        5   "C" "
        6   "D" "
        7   Transport Officer & Q.M.
        8   8th R. War. R.
        9   Orderly Room.

Copy No. 2

Reference OPERATION ORDER NO. 34.

ADDITIONS & AMENDMENTS.

Para. 8. BOMBING PARTIES.

"The colours of this Battn. will be red and yellow".

(Sgd) J.L.MELLOR, Captain,

Adjutant for O.C. 1/6 R.War

26/6/16.

Further Amendments to Operation Order 34.

ARTILLERY LIFT.   Artillery will lift off the objective
of 8th. R.War.R. at 0.20 not 0.15

SPECIAL PARTIES. (i) Parties of 1st. Somerset L.I. &
1st. Hants. will time their attack so
that they arrive at the guns by 1.15
hours at which hour the artillery will
lift from the guns.
(ii) As the above gun parties advance
the special patrols told off to cut
wire will move simultaneously.

DIVIDING LINE.   Between 1st. Somerset L.I. and 6th.
R.War.R. should read:-
K 35 d 4.9. K 36 c 3.6 both points
inclusive to Somerset L.I.

OBJECTIVE.   Final objective of the 11th. Brigade
is to capture and consolidate the
line
Q 6 c 9.3. Q 6 c 9.3. (new trench)
K 36 c 3.5, K 36 a 8.2.

CONTACT PATROL   As per attached.

23/8/16.   (Sgd) J.L.MELLOR, Captain,
                        Adjutant for O.C. 1/6 R.War.R.

Reference OPERATION ORDER NO. 34 Para. 7.

7. CONTACT AEROPLANE PATROLS.

The following instructions are issued:-

"During the coming attack it is hoped to have one contact aeroplane always up. This aeroplane has been specially warned to look out for flares at the following hours:-

    Between 0.20 and 0.30
        "   1.20 and 1.30
        "   1.50 and 2.00 (to be lit only by troops detailed to attack PENDANT COPSE & PENDANT TRENCH)
        "   3.30 and 4.00.

Flares will be lit at these hours by leading troops at whatever point they may have arrived at.

The flares when lighted should as far as possible be placed in such a position as to be visible not only from the air, but also from observation posts along the line AUCHONVILLERS - SUCRERIE - PYLON AVENUE.

2. In addition, the 11th. Brigade will light flares on arrival at the 2nd. objective.

3. The magnesium lights which have been recently issued are only to be used after all the red flares have been expended.

                      Lieut. Colonel,

                      General Staff, 4th. Division.

OPERATION ORDER NO 37 ISSUED BY LIEUT. COL. W.H. FRANKLIN
COMMANDING 1/6 ROYAL WARWICKSHIRE REGIMENT.   COPY NO 2.

JUNE 26th 1916.

1. C & D Companies less Brigade Carrying Party and Stokes Gun Carrying Party will take over Sector of the front line today.

2. Major F.H. Deakin will be in command.

3. The Sector is from SERRE ROAD exclusive to the end of trench 35/4 inclusive.

4. Companies will parade outside their billets fully equipped and armed for the day of the assault, at 3.30 pm.

5. D. Company will move off by platoons at 250 yards distance. Four platoon guides will meet them at LYCEUM at 5.0 p.m.

6. C. Company will follow "D" Coy. Guides will meet them at the Junction of STERLING STREET and CHEERHO AVENUE.

7. O.C. "D" Coy. will detail responsible N.C.O. to take over stores at the Hd. Qrs. 1st R. War. R. at 4-0 p.m.

8. Cpl. Hook will take over Signalling Stores from 1st R. War.R. at the LYCEUM at 4-0p.m.

9. "D" Coy. will take over posts held by "C" Coy. 1st R. War.R.

10. No dixies will be taken all cooking done in mess-tins.

11. All men's packs and Officers' valises will be outside the present Coy. Hd. Qrs. by 2-0 p.m. from where they will be collected by the Transport at that time.

12. Greatcoats, also rations for Tuesday, will be carried loose.

13. Men of Carrying Party belonging to "C" Coy. will be attached to "A" Coy. and those of "D" Coy. attached to "B" Coy.

     (Signed) J.L. MELLOR,
     CAPT. & ADJT. for
     O/C 1/6th R. Warwicks. Regt.

Issued at 11-0 a.m.

Copy No.	1	To file.	Copy No.	6	To "D" Coy.
" "	2	War Diary.	" "	7	Q.M.
" "	3	"A" Coy.	" "	8	Transport Officer.
" "	4	"B" "	" "	9	Regt. Sgt. Major.
" "	5	"C" "	" "	10	Office.

OPERATION ORDER NO. 38 BY LIEUT. COL. W.H. FRANKLIN
COMMANDING 1/6 R.WAR.R.

COPY NO. 2

June 26th. 1916.

1. The Battalion less C & D Coys. will move to cellar billets on MAILLY-MAILLET this evening.

2. Companies will fall in, B Coy. leading then A. Coy., with the head of leading Coy. outside B Coys most easterly billet

3. They will proceed by platoons marching at 250 yards distance with connecting files. First platoon moving at 8-0 p.m.

4. Dress: Fully armed and equipped for the day of assault and packs.

5. Lewis Guns and full complement of magazines in buckets will be carried.

6. Cookers will accompany companies.

7. All officer's kits and Orderly Room boxes to be outside Battn. H.Q. at 7-15 p.m.

8. All transport and Q.M. Stores will move to billets and lines allotted in BERTRANCOURT.

9. No officers will be mounted.

10. Transport Officer will make special arrangements for removing the balance of transport to BERTRANCOURT.

11. All ranks are specially warned that they must remain in cellars unless detailed for duties.

(Sgd) J.L. MELLOR, Captain,
Adjutant for O.C. 1/6 R.War.R.

Issued at 2-0 p.m.

Copy No. 1.	File.
" " 2.	War Diary.
" " 3.	O.C. "A" Coy.
" " 4.	" "B" "
" " 5.	" "C" "
" " 6.	" "D" "
" " 7	Quartermaster.
" " 8	Transport Officer.
" " 9	Regt. Sergt. Major.
" " 10	Office.

OPERATION ORDER NO' 39 BY LIEUT. COL. W.H.FRANKLIN   COPY No. 2
       COMMANDING 1/6 R.WAR.R.
                                          JUNE 28th. 1916.

1. The 8th. R.War.R. will relieve the garrison holding the front line by 10-0 p.m.

2. C & D Companies will move into their assembly trenches or Legend by 11-45 p.m.

3. C & D Coy's greatcoats should be stored in Batt. H.Qrs. or in another dug-out by 11-30 p.m. Major Deakin will detail a man who will remain with them.

4. H.Qrs. and A. & B Coys will pass the Railway Crossing on MAILLY MAILLET -SUCRERIE Road at 10#40 p.m. battalion to be clear by 10-55 p.m.

5. Route: Up main SUCRERIE Road (or just on left side of it) to SUCRERIE. Thence Battalion may march across country or down SERRE Road until 12 midnight. Any of our Artillery which might prove dangerous have been ordered not to fire up to that hour.

6. Formation: Platoons at 250 yards distance with connecting files - H.Qrs. - A Coy. - B Coy.

7. Stokes Gun Carriers are to move under orders of Lieut. LEWER.

8. Companies may send small party to their assembly ~~trenches~~ ahead position by day.

9. Report is to be made to Battn. H.Qrs which will be forwarded to Brigade H.Qrs. at LYCEUM as soon as each Company is in its Assembly Trenches.

10. Brigade ~~objective~~ H.Qrs. remains at LYCEUM until the Brigade objective has been taken when it will move to about P94. LYCEUM will remain open as report centre all day.

11. No smoking or lights will be permitted after the Battalion has paraded to march off from billets. The strictest silence will be observed during the march
All ranks will take the greatest care not to disclose to the enemy the fact that our positions of assembly have been occupied.

                                        (Sgd) J.L.MELLOR, Captain,
                                         Adjutant for O.C. 1/6 R.War.R.

Issued at 10-0 a.m.

Copy No.			Copy No.		
" " 1	File		" " 9	Signals (Lt. K.Brown)	
" " 2	War Diary		" " 10	Lt. E.D.Moore.	
" " 3	O.C. "A" Copy.		" " 11	Q.M. & Transport O.	
" " 4	" "B" "		" " 12	Grenade O. Lt. Baxter.	
" " 5	" "C" "		" " 13	8th. R.War.R.	
" " 6	" "D" "		" " 14	Medical Officer.	
" " 7	Commanding Officer.		" " 15	Office.	
" " 8	2nd. in Command.		" " 16	Spare.	

Amendments to Operation Order No. 39.

1. Each company will be outside its company H.Qrs ready to move off at 10-10 p.m. Signallers and runners outside Battalion H.Qrs.

2. Head of the Battalion to pass the starting point by 10-30 – not 10-40 p.m. and to be clear of same by 10-55 p.m.

3. Order of march – H.Qrs – A, B, C & D Coys connecting forward. A Coy. will detail guide to H.Qrs.

4. After reaching point where CHEERHOH Trench cuts the EUSTON – AUCHONVILLERS Road – it is propsed to go along the northern edge of CHEERHOH as far as BELFRY TRENCH.

30/6/16.

(Sgd) J.L.MELLOR, Captain,
Adjutant for O.C. 1/5 R.War.R

1/6th ROYAL WARWICKSHIRE REGT.

COPY NO. 2.

SECRET.

OPERATION ORDER No. 31.

Reference Map 57/10&000.

No. 1. Battalion will move, as part of the Brigade into bivouacs at COUIN on the morning of the 31st. inst.,

2. Battalion will take over the same hutments as they occupied on the 25th inst.

3. Head of the Battalion will be at Bridge A 27 C 54, facing South, ready to move at 3.55 a.m., and will move in the following order:- Signallers, A. B. C. & D. All Headquarters Company, less Signallers, will form up as a party, and march in rear of the battalion.

4. "C" Coy. will detail one Officer and six men to march in rear of the whole Brigade Column from the starting point A.22 B.79.

5. The two spare cooks not marching with Company Cookers, will fall in with Headquarters Company, referred to in paragraph 3.

6. 8 Breaksmen will be detailed by the Adjutant — two per Company — these men will consist of men most unlikely to withstand the march, and Company Commanders should have these names ready in the morning.

7. A halt will be made for Breakfast about 6.30 a.m.

8. All Officer's kits and mess boxes to be ready outside "A" Co mess by 3 o'clock.

9. A G.S. Wagon and Limber will call at HdQrs. at 3 o'clock for all surplus stores, Officer's valises and mess boxes (2 per Co being allowed), and will then call for Co Officers kits at "A" Co's mess at 3.15 a.m.

10. Mounted Officers' Horses will be ready at 3.30 a.m.

May 30th 1916.

2/nd Lt. & A/Adjt, for
O.C. 1/6th Bn. R.War.R.

Copy No. 1. To file.
2 " War Diary.
3 " "A"
4 " "B"
5 " "C"
6 " "D"
7 " Headquarters.
8 " Transport Officer.
9 " Quartermaster.
10 " Sergeant Major

ISSUED TO

No.	
1	To File.
2	War Diary.
3	O.C. " A " Coy.
4	" " B " "
5	" " C " "
6	" " D " "
7	Commanding Officer.
8	2nd in Command.
9	Signals Lieut. K. Brown.
10	Carrying Party, Lieut. A.D. Moore.
11	Q.M. & Transport Officer.
12	Grenades Officer, Lieut. Baxter.
13	8th R. Warwicks. Regt.
14	Medical Officer.
15	Office.
16	Spare.

ADDITIONS & AMENDMENTS TO OPERATION ORDER NO. 34.

1. SMOKE. The evening discharges of smoke on X and Y days are cancelled, otherwise all arrangements the same.
B.M. 990.

2. PREPARING WIRE. This will be commenced on W/X night NOT on X/Y night as stated. Major Deakin will detail parties from Support Platoons as soon as he arrives in trenches on W/X night. If in his opinion further assistance is needed for X/Y night, early application must be made to C.O.
The wire must not only be cut but cleared completely.
2/Lt. A.E. Chowil's place has been taken by 2/Lt. W.P. Wheeler.

3. CONTACT AEROPLANES. During the coming attack it is hoped to leave one contact patrol aeroplane always up. Flares should be placed in such a position whenever possible as to be visible not only from the air but also from the O.P.'s along the general line AUCHONVILLERS - SUCRERIE - PYLON AVENUE.
Hours at which flares are to be lighted in 11th Bde. Area:-
(a) 0.20 after arrival at first objective.
(b) 0.45 "   "   "   " second   "
(c) 1.15 by party detailed to capture guns.
Aeroplane may not see these flares but they could probably be seen from ROWLAND RIDGE.

4. ROYAL ENGINEERS. When the Battn. reaches its objective and the Bde. has been advised, half a section of Durham R.E. will be sent
B.M. 993.
to Point 63 to help consolidate. The Battn. will ration the half section (about 18 men) on Z night.

5. BOMBING PARTIES. Bombing Parties of 31st Div. will carry Red Flags - those of this Battn. These must always be carried not fixed.

6. IDENTITY DISCS. Triangular Pieces of Tin are to be worn by all assaulting troops. Those Coys. in the line will fix theirs as well as possible during Y/Z night. They are to be fixed to haversacks. These will not be worn by carriers, runners, signallers, stretcher bearers, ration parties or anyone detailed to go to the rear.

7. BATTALION HEADQUARTERS. During Y/Z night these will be in a dug-out in LEGEND TRENCH.

8. WATER. The garrison in trenches is responsible that sufficient water is stored for all men to make tea whilst in assembly trenches. It should be stored by the afternoon of X day and placed under guard. Biscuit Tins will be sent up.

9. WATER TINS & RUNNERS. These must always be returned to dump - the supply is short and the issue of water is dependant on this order being carefully carried out.

10. CASUALTIES. Coy. Commanders must send in returns once every 2 hrs.

11. ELECTRIC TORCHES. Must be carried by all in possession of them.

12. GARRISON. The 2 Coys. moving up on W day should go fully equipped for 2 day. In addition they will carry in sandbags rations for X day and greatcoats which will be dumped in a dug-out on Y/Z night, also five dixies per coy.

13. STOKES CARRIERS. An additional ten men will be detailed 2 from "A" & "C" Coys. 3 from "B" & "D" Coys.

14. DIVIDING LINES. Between 1/Somerset Light Infy. & 6th R. War.R. should read K 36 c 2.7, not K 36 c 3.2.

J.L. MELLOR,
CAPT. & ADJT. for
O/C 4/6th R. Warwicks. Regt.

Copy..........

SECRET

1/6th BATTALION ROYAL WARWICKSHIRE REGT.   Copy No. 2

Ref: Sheet 57D N.E.1/20,000   OPERATION ORDER No. 32.

1. The Battalion will relieve 5th R. War. R. in 8 section trenches to-morrow the 8th inst.

2. Battalion will parade in the following order:-
   A Coy. move off at 6.50 a.m.
   B   "   "   " " 6.55 a.m.
   D   "   "   " " 7.0 a.m.
   C   "   "   " " 7.5 a.m.
   Hdqrs "   "   "   7.10 a.m.

3. A & B Companies will be in the firing line - A on the right, B on the left. C Company will take over billets in SAILLY in reserve. D Company will take over billets in HEBUTERNE AND BE IN SUPPORT.

4. All troops will proceed by the valley road, moving by sections at 50 yards distance. Vehicles will proceed at distance of 200 yards. In order to lessen the amount of transport on the road, baggage wagons of incoming battalions will be used to carry out baggage of outgoing battalions.

5. All officers kits and mess boxes will be ready stacked outside Orderly Room at 6.30 a.m. Cookers to be ready by 6.30 a.m.

6. Lewis Gun Officer will be responsible for movement of Lewis Guns

7. All tents are to be carefully cleaned before leaving the lines.

8. Guides from each platoon of A, B and D Coys of the 5th Batt. will be at cross roads K.15.A.9.9. at 8.30 a.m. to lead Companies to their positions

                                        2/Lieut. & A/Adjt.,
7/6/16.   for O/C 1/6th R. War. R.

   Copy. No. 1   To file   Copy No. 6   D
          2   War Diary   7   Headquarters
          3   A   8   Transport Officer
          4   B   9   Quartermaster
          5   C   10   Sergeant Major.

48

D.A.G.
G.H.Q.
3rd, LONDON.

Appendix 6 May 15

WAR DIARIES.

The enclosed copies of Operation Orders should have been forwarded to with the War Diary for May.

Please add to May 28th. "Reinforcements 54", which was inadvertently omitted.

20/6/15.

Captain & Adjutant,
For O.C. 1/6 B. War D.

143rd Inf.Bde.
48th Div.

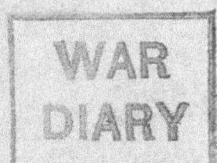

1/6th BATTN. THE ROYAL WARWICKSHIRE REGIMENT.

J U L Y

1 9 1 6

Attached:

Battn. O.O. No. 40.

Army Form C. 2118.

1/6th R W☒ R WAR DIARY July 1916
INTELLIGENCE SUMMARY.
(Erase heading not required.)

Place	Date	Hour	Summary of Events and Information	Remarks and references to Appendices
MAILLY	1	7.40 a.m.	Battalion left their assembly trenches 10 mins behind the 1/8th R War R - heavy casualties about 80 before crossing our own lines - many led with 1/8th R War R immediately on reaching German lines - worked up on the third line - first and second wave Battalions on the right had advanced no further - 31st Division on left also hung up certain units reaching SERRE - Enemy's opposition a well disiplined barrage and very severe cross machine gun fire - 12th Inf Bde followed but were unable to advance further than line held by 11th Inf Bde The no officer unhit (2/Lt J S Cooper) returned with a message to Brigade HQ between 11 and 12 a.m. The line which was being consolidated was severely pressed on its flanks and forced to withdraw to the Quadrilateral from where the few remaining men were sent back to our lines about Y.h.m. All that could be collected were taken back to MAILLY at midnight. Estimated Casualties 120 Killed & Missing 316 Wounded. Officers Killed. Capt. A.B.RABONE 2/Lieut J. BALKWILL 2/Lieuts S J WINKLEY HLFIELD - R V ROSE. 2Lt J E B DIXON - 2/Lt R C MARTIN HLFIELD - R V ROSE. 2/Lt W P WHEELER - 2/Lt R R RICE - 2/Lt C T MORRIS DAVIES Missing believed Killed 2/Lt A E CLARKE Wounded and Missing 2/Lt Col W H FRANKLIN - Maj F H DEAKIN - Capts A B TURNER Wounded 2Lt Col W H FRANKLIN - Maj F H DEAKIN - Capts A B TURNER J N G STAFFORD - F W JONES - Lieuts A D WILCOX - WHB BAXTER - K BROWN F L MORGAN - 2/Lieut A N DOWNING - K HERNE	J/M

Army Form C.2118.

WAR DIARY
or
INTELLIGENCE SUMMARY.

(Erase heading not required.)

1/6" R. War. R

July 1916

Instructions regarding War Diaries and Intelligence Summaries are contained in F.S. Regs., Part II. and the Staff Manual respectively. Title pages will be prepared in manuscript.

Place	Date	Hour	Summary of Events and Information	Remarks and references to Appendices
MAILLY	2.7.16		In billets - gradually assembling - until total of 176 reached. Reinforcement of 5 Route Officers from Duke of Cornwalls L.I. - 2/Lieut J.W. HIGMAN - 2/Lt O.W. BASETT - 2/Lt D.W. TONKING - 2/Lt G. CHELE - 2/Lt J. LOMAX	J.S.M.
COUIN	3.7.16		Marched from 11th Brigade to join 143rd Inf Bde in bivouac at COUIN joined (Reserve Army)	J.S.M.
	4.7.16		In bivouac. Reinforcement 6 O.R.	J.S.M.
	5.7.16		Reinforcement 14 O.R. and 2Lieut H S POWELL	J.S.M.
	6.7.16		Capt L.C. Crocheford rejoined for duty	J.S.M.
	7.7.16		Major F.J. DANIELSEN took over command	J.S.M.
	8.7.16		In Corps Reserve	J.S.M.
	9.7.16		"	J.S.M.
	10.7.16		2/Lt HOLLAND and 2/Lt RHODES temporarily attached from 1/4" R WAR. 2/Lt THOMPSON, 2/Lt W.B. LYCETT + Lt R.H. G BATTEN temporarily attached from 5th Glos	J.S.M.
	11.7.16		Lt R.S. PARTRIDGE joined for duty. Reinforcement O.R. 78	J.S.M.
	12.7.16		"	J.S.M.
ALBERT	13.7.16		Brigade moved to west side of ALBERT by motor bus - marched to bivouac on Eastern side. Attached to 25th Division.	J.S.M.
ALBERT	14.7.16		In Bivouac. Found carrying parties. 2/Lt H. BURTON + 2/Lt W.A. WAGNER of 3rd S. Staffs R. 2/Lt T. WHEELDON - 4th QUEENS R joined for duty (R West Surrey R) Reinforcement 126 O.R.	J.S.M.

Army Form C. 2118.

Instructions regarding War Diaries and Intelligence Summaries are contained in F.S. Regs., Part II. and the Staff Manual respectively. Title pages will be prepared in manuscript.

WAR DIARY or INTELLIGENCE SUMMARY

1/6th R W Surr   July 1916

(Erase heading not required.)

Place	Date	Hour	Summary of Events and Information	Remarks and references to Appendices
ALBERT	15th		In Bivouac	JWM
"	16th		Relieved 2nd Royal Irish Rifles in trenches S.E. of OVILLERS - 2 Companies in front - two in support. 2/Lt B. L. JAMES - 2/Lt B.J.W.PURCHASE - T. RUDDOCK of 3/4th BUFFS (East Kent Reg) joined for duty	JWM
"	17th		In Trenches. Two bombing attacks - pushed forward 200 yds - Casualties 2/Lt BATTEN wounded. 1 K. 22 W. of O.R. - Reinforcement 1. O.R.	JWM
"	18th		In Trenches. Casualties 4 K. 25 W. of O.R. Reinforcement 27 O.R. and 17 Officers Capt. W.S. FISHER. 4th Nottauts. 2/Lt C.J. MYERS. 2/Lt F.H.RUST. 2/Lt A.J.B. PEARSON. 2/Lt R.A. STEPHENSON. 2/Lt W.V. SHELTON. 2/Lt H.C. WILLIAMS. 5th Essex. 2/Lt A.J.S. Grant 4th Essex - 2/Lt A.P. HAGGO. 4th R Scots Fus. 2/Lt L.B. SHAW. LAWRENCE 2/Lt J. CHALCROFT. 2/Lt H.F. ALSOP. 2/Lt C.J. CROCKETT. 2/Lt C.F. SEDDON. 2/Lt W.S. CATTELL. 2/Lt H. SKILLINGTON 4th Nottauts	JWM
"	19th		Relieved by 1/5th Glos R. Casualties 3 K. 16 W. of O.R. 2/Lt JAMES. Wounded - marched to billets at BOUZINCOURT.	JWM
BOUZINCOURT	20th		Reinforcement 50. O.R.	JWM
"	21st		In Billets.	JWM
"	22nd		" 119 O.R.	JWM

620

Army Form C. 2118.

WAR DIARY
or
INTELLIGENCE SUMMARY.

1/6 R War   July 1916

(Erase heading not required.)

Place	Date	Hour	Summary of Events and Information	Remarks and references to Appendices
BOUZINCOURT	23		In Billets in Divisional Reserve — Moved up at 9.30 p.m. to support Trenches between OVILLERS and AVELUY. (Ref. W1.8.d.2.8.)	J.A.M.
AVELUY	24		In Reserve — Found carrying parties. Casualties 2 O.R. wounded	J.A.M.
"	25		" 2/Lt POWELL wounded but remained at duty 4 O.R. "	J.A.M.
"	26		" Joined X Corps moved to closer trenches between OVILLERS & BOISELLE (X14 a.6.4)	J.A.M.
BOISELLE	27		" Relieved about 6 p.m by 4th Royal SUSSEX - marched to Billets in BOUZINCOURT. Casualties 3 O.R. wounded Reinforcement 67 O.R	J.A.M.
"	28		Moved to Billets at MAISON ROLLAND by motor bus. Rejoined X Corps.	J.A.M.
MAISON ROLLAND	29		At Rest in Billets	J.A.M.
"	30		In Billets Reorganisation and Training	J.A.M.
"	31		" " Reinforcement 130 O.R.	J.A.M.

F.S. Drummond Lt Col
Commdg 1/6 Bn R War R

BATTALION OPERATION ORDER NO. 40.

Operation Order No 40
O.C. 1/6th by R War R

1. The 6th & 8th R War R will rejoin their 143rd Brigade at Couin today

2. The Battalion will fall in ready to march off at 3.55 p.m - head of the column opposite the Town Major's office

3. Order of March Sig & Orderlies - A B C D - Companies to march at 5 mins interval

4. Dress - Fighting Order

5. Route Beaussart - Bertrancourt Bus Couin

6. All valises - mess boxes etc to be in push way of billet 20 at 3 p.m

3/7/16

J L Miller / Capt
O C 1/6th R War R

143rd Brigade.
48th Division

1/6th BATTALION

ROYAL WARWICKSHIRE REGIMENT

AUGUST 1 9 1 6

Army Form C. 2118.

1/6ᵗʰ R. War R WAR DIARY Aug 1916
or INTELLIGENCE SUMMARY.
(Erase heading not required.)

Place	Date	Hour	Summary of Events and Information	Remarks and references to Appendices
MAISON ROLLAND	1/8		In Billets. Training. Capt. B. HARGREAVE joined for duty 31/7/16	J.d.M.
	2nd		Lieut. A. POYNTING attached 143 M.G.C. killed 26/7/16	J.d.M.
	3rd		Capt. T.H. LAWLEY joined for duty 1/8/16	J.d.M.
	4th		Reinforcement 8 O.R.	J.d.M.
	5th		"	J.d.M.
	6th		"	J.d.M.
	7th		Reinforcement 5 O.R.	J.d.M.
	8th		2/Lt BURTON 3rd S.Staffs transferred to 1/7ᵗʰ R. War R	J.d.M.
GEZAINCOURT	9th		Brigade marched to GEZAINCOURT	J.d.M.
LEALVILLERS	10th		Brigade marched to LEALVILLERS. Reinforcement 48 O.R.	J.d.M.
	11th		In Training.	J.d.M.
	12th		" 2/Lt. BELCHER F.T.J. 25ᵗʰ C. of London joined for duty	J.d.M.
	13th		" 2/Lt A.E. CLARKE confirmed as prisoner.	J.d.M.
BOUZINCOURT	14th		Battalion marched to bivouac at BOUZINCOURT Reinforcement 2 O.R.	J.d.M.
	15th		In bivouac. Training.	J.d.M.
OVILLERS	16th		Relieved 1/4ᵗʰ Gloucester Regt in sector between OVILLERS and THIEPVAL - 1/7ᵗʰ R. War R on our left - 1/4ᵗʰ Oxfords on our right. Casualties O.R 3. Killed 10 Wounded.	J.d.M.

Army Form C. 2118.

Instructions regarding War Diaries and Intelligence Summaries are contained in F. S. Regs., Part II. and the Staff Manual respectively. Title pages will be prepared in manuscript.

1/6th R.War.R WAR DIARY Aug. 1916
or
INTELLIGENCE SUMMARY.
(Erase heading not required.)

Place	Date	Hour	Summary of Events and Information	Remarks and references to Appendices
OVILLERS	17th		In trenches - Counter attack attempted by Hun on right but stopped by the artillery. Casualties 2/Lt B.J.W. PURCHASE wounded. 2/Lt A.PHASGO slightly wounded but remained at duty. O.R. 3 Killed 11 Wounded	JLM
	18th		In trenches. Took part in attack with 1/6th R.War.R - 4th R.Berk.R co-operated on right. Held up for short time on right by German strong post but soon succeeded in taking whole objective capturing 6 Officers and 245 O.R including large numbers of N.C.Os. - Casualties Capt. R.C.LOWE. 2/Lt A.J.B.PEARSON - 2/Lt C.J.CROCKETT - 2/Lt H.S.SKILLINGTON - 2/Lt SEDDON. 2/Lt A.PHASGO. Killed. Capt B.HARGREAVE - 2/Lt SEDDON. 2/Lt SHELTON wounded. O.R. 23 Killed. 90 W. 10 Missing.	JLM
"	19th.		In trenches. Consolidating captured territory. Casualties O.R. 3 Killed 10 Wounded 2 Missing. Moved slightly to left at night.	JLM
	20th.		Consolidating until 3 p.m. when relieved by 1/7th Worcester Reg. moved to bivouac at BOUZINCOURT. Casualties O.R. 3 Killed y Wounded Reinforcement 8 O.R.	JLM
BOUZINCOURT	21st		In Bivouac. Resting. Reinforcement 35 O.R	JLM
"	22nd		In Bivouac	JLM
OVILLERS	2.23rd		Battalion moved to OVILLERS - 2 Companies & No.2. at USNA-REDOUBT and 2 companies in support trenches in OVILLERS. - Casualties 2/Lt C.F. SEDDON and 2/Lt W.S. CATTELL - slight shell shock. O.R. 6 wounded	JLM

Army Form C. 2118.

1/6th War R WAR DIARY Aug 1916
or
INTELLIGENCE SUMMARY.

(Erase heading not required.)

Instructions regarding War Diaries and Intelligence Summaries are contained in F. S. Regs., Part II. and the Staff Manual respectively. Title pages will be prepared in manuscript.

Place	Date	Hour	Summary of Events and Information	Remarks and references to Appendices
OVILLERS	24th		Relieved 1/5th R.WAR.R in trenches north of OVILLERS — Casualties O.R 4 Killed 7 Wounded	J2h 9th
"	25th		In trenches. Casualties O.R 4 Killed 6 Wounded	J2h 9th
"	26th		Relieved by 1/4 R War R and moved to bivouac at BOUZINCOURT. Casualties O.R 1 Killed 6 Wounded	J2h 9th
BOUZINCOURT	27th		Resting. Reinforcement 22 O.R	J2h
VARENNES	28th		Marched to Hutments at Varennes. 2/Lt J HARRISON & 2/Lt SE BOWDEN (5th Batt Devon Rgt) joined for duty	J2h 9th
WARNEMONT	29th		and at G.H.Q. EASTERBROOK (5th Batt. Devon Rgt) joined for duty Marched to Hutments in BOIS de WARNEMONT.	J2h 9th
"	30th		Training.	9th
"	31st			9th

JW Mellor/Major.
Commanding 1/6th R War R.

Copy No 2   11

           Operation Order No 42
               by Lt. Col F. B. Danielsen
                  commanding 1/6th R War R.

Ref Trench Map 1/5000. (OVILLERS)   18. 8. 16

1. The ~~opn~~ battalion will take part in
   an attack with the 1/5th R War R. at 5 p.m.

2. The objectives are in X 2 b.
      First   Point 62 inclusive to 20 exclusive
      Second   Points 55 and 44.
      Third   Points 59. 48. and 06.

3. D. Co will attack the first and second
   objectives – C. Co the final objective and
   if possible C Co will push up to R 32 d 1.2
   and R 32 c 9.1.

4. B. Co will ~~accompany~~ attack one platoon
   each to C & D Cos to carry tools
   and sandbags. – also a party of 20 to
   143 T. M. B. to carry ammunition.
   Remainder of B. Co will be between
   points 47 and 77. A. Co in reserve between
   points 44 and 10.

5. ~~5.~~
5. Batt. H.Q. will be near point 47.

Copy No 2.   13

6. All assaulting troops will be equipped as lightly as possible.

7. Every man will carry 2 No 5 bombs and 2 sandbags — carrying party 2 tools and 5 sandbags.

8. Section of 143 T.M.B. between points 26-47 will be in readiness to move forward. Medium and Heavy Mortars have been allotted targets.

9. Artillery programme and issue of smoke have been explained to all company commanders.

10. All up traffic is to be from Point 10 to 44 - 47 - 90 — down traffic 20-26 - 02 X2c92 - X8b88

11. All objectives taken are to be immediately consolidated and held.

                                    J.P. Hare
                                    2nd Lt & a/Adj
By Orderly
  1 p.m.

OPERATION ORDER NO. 41 BY LT. Col. F.G. DANIELSEN COMMANDING

1/6 R. WAR. REGT.　　　　　　　　　　　AUGUST 13/1916.

Ref. Sheet 11 (Lens)　　　　　　　　　　　　Copy No. 1....

1. Battalion will move to BOULAINCOURT tomorrow where the Brigade will be in Divisional Reserve.

2. Coys. will parade with the head of the column opposite Billet 90 facing up the hill ready to move at 7-40 a.m. Dress: Full marching order.

3. Order of march: Signallers, D,C,B,A Coys.

4. A Company will find I Officer and 8 men for rear party to march in rear of transport. Also 8 men as brakesmen to report to Transport Officer at 7-30 a.m

5. All water bottles will be filled tonight.

6. Officers kits and mess boxes to be in Billet 73 yard by 6-45 a.m.

7. Lights Out will be at 9-30 pm. tonight. Mn to be in billets by 9-0 p.m.

8. O.C.Coys. will hand to Adjutant prior to moving off a certificate shewing Nos. of Offrs.,NCOs and Other Ranks on parade Also a certificate shewing that billets and latrines have been left in a cleanly condition.

　　　　　　　　　(Sgd) G.C.HELE, 2/Lt.

　　　　　　　　　A/ Adjutant, 1/6 R.War.Regt.

Issued by Orderly at 7-45 p.m.

　　Copy No. 1. File.
　　"   " 2. War Diary
　　"   " 3. O.C. A Coy.
　　"   " 4. " B "
　　"   " 5. " C "
　　"   " 6. " D "
　　"   " 7 Transport Offr. & Qartermaster.
　　"   " 8. Headquarters.

48th. DIVISION

143rd INFANTRY BDE.

1/6th. ROYAL WARWICKSHIRE REGT.

SEPTEMBER 1916.

Army Form C. 2118.

1/6th R War R WAR DIARY September 1916
or INTELLIGENCE SUMMARY.
(Erase heading not required.)

Place	Date	Hour	Summary of Events and Information	Remarks and references to Appendices
WARNEMONT	1/9		In Bivouac	9d m
AUCHELLES	2/9		Marched to huttments at Vauchelles	9d m
"	3/9		In training	9d m
"	4/9		Reinforcement 5 O.R.	9d m
"	5/9		Inspected by G O C 48th Div.	9d m
"	6/9		Visited by Gen. Sir H de la P. Gough KCB. Comg Reserve Army	9d m
"	7/9		"	9d m
"	8/9		"	9d m
"	9/9		2/Lieut C F SEDDON rejoined for duty	9d m
"	10/9		Draft O R 24.	9d m
GEZINCOURT	11/9		Battalion marched as part of the Brigade across country to new billets at GEZINCOURT.	9d m
"	12/9		Training	9d m
"	13/9		Reinforcement O R 10.	9d m
"	14/9		"	9d m
"	15/9		Reinforcement O R 12 & Capt. J. BOWATER	9d m
"	16/9		"	9d m

1577 Wt.W10791/1773 500,000 1/15 D. D. & L. A.D.S.S./Forms/C. 2118.

Army Form C. 2118.

1/6 R War R WAR DIARY September 1916
INTELLIGENCE SUMMARY.

(Erase heading not required.)

Place	Date	Hour	Summary of Events and Information	Remarks and references to Appendices
GEZAINCOURT	17/9		In Training Honours Military Cross awarded to Capt. A C CROCKFORD and 2.C.M. to 24535 Cpl J.V HASELER.	J.J.M
"	18/9		Marched to Billets at PROUVILLE Reinforcement 27 O.R.	J.J.M
PROUVILLE	18/9		In Training Reinforcement & Officers 4th Cheshire Regt.	
"	19/9		Capt. E.R JOHNSTON 2/Lt. G.H DRAPER 2/Lt J B MUSGRAVE.	J.J.M
			7th Cheshire Regt. Capt. G LINFOOT. Capt. H A LINFOOT 2Lt CH.B.SEEL.	
			Lieut F A GODWIN 2/Lt R B W GOSSE	
	20/9		In Training Re-inforcement. 6 O.R	J.J.M
	21/9		"	J.J.M
	22/9		"	J.J.M
	23/9		"	J.J.M
	24/9		" 7 O R	J.J.M
	25/9		"	J.J.M
	26/9		"	J.J.M
	27/9 & 28/9		" 32 O.R 108 O.R	J.J.M
MONDECOURT	29/9		Marched to Billets at MONDECOURT 7 O.R Reinforcement 64 O.R	J.J.M
BAYENCOURT	30/9		" " " at BAYENCOURT Capt F.R. JOHNSTON transferred to 15th RUS.	J.J.M

F J Smain Lt Colonel
1/6 R War R

Army Form C. 2118.

WAR DIARY or INTELLIGENCE SUMMARY

1/6th R War R

October

(Erase heading not required.)

Vol 20

Place	Date	Hour	Summary of Events and Information	Remarks and references to Appendices
BAYENCOURT	1/10		In Billets - Finding Working Parties in Hebuterne Sector	J d h
"	2/10		- A Co attached to 1/5th R War R - Reinforcement 2 O R	J d h
"	3/10		"	J d h
CHATEAU LA HAIE	4/10		HQ & 3 Companies moved to CHATEAU LA HAIE	J d h
ST AMAND	5/10		moved to billets at ST AMAND. A Co rejoined the Battalion. Training	J d h
"	6/10		"	J d h
"	7/10		2/Lieut F.Y. Surman & 6 O R. Reinforcement	J d h
"	8/10		"	J d h
"	9/10			J d h
"	10/10		Reinforcement 4 O R	J d h
"	11/10			J d h
HEBUTERNE	12/10		Relieved 1/4th Berks Regt in HEBUTERNE left sector - one company in line, one in HEBUTERNE. - HQ & 2 Co in FONQUEVILLERS. Attached 144 Inf Bde	J d h
"	13/10		In Trenches Casualties 1 Killed 4 Wounded (of which 3 died later) O R	J d h
"	14/10		In Trenches Casualties 2 Killed 3 Wounded	J d h
"	15/10		In Trenches	J d h
ST AMAND	16/10		Relieved by 1/6th Gloucester Regt moved to billets at ST AMAND. Rejoined 143 Inf Bde	J d h

1577 Wt.W10791/1773 500,000 1/15 D.D.&L. A.D.S.S./Forms/C. 2118.

Army Form C. 2118.

WAR DIARY
or
1/6th R W Fus R INTELLIGENCE SUMMARY. October 1916

(Erase heading not required.)

Place	Date	Hour	Summary of Events and Information	Remarks and references to Appendices
ST AMAND	17/10		In Billets.	J.L.M.
"	18/10		Training. Reinforcement 8. O.R.	J.L.M.
"	19/10		Training. Military Medal awarded to No 2583 Pte C. V. Taylor	J.L.M.
Grande ROULLECOURT	20/10		Marched to billets at GRAND ROULLECOURT. Reinforcement O.R. 1.	J.L.M.
"	21/10		Training. Reinforcement 5. O.R	J.L.M.
"	22/10		" Military Medal awarded to No 20262 A/Cpl G Tulip + No 10290 Pte F Deakin. both	J.L.M.
"	23/10		Reinforcement 5. O.R (late of 2nd Worcs Regt.	J.L.M.
"	24/10		"	J.L.M.
BAIZIEUX	25/10		Moved by motor to Camp at BAIZIEUX	J.L.M.
BECOURT	26/10		Marched to Camp at BECOURT	J.L.M.
MAMETZ	27/10		Marched to Camp at MAMETZ WOOD - Found working parties on roads	J.L.M.
"	28/10		Finding large working parties on roads. Reinforcement 4. O.R	J.L.M.
"	29/10		"	J.L.M.
"	30/		"	J.L.M.
"	31/		"	J.L.M.

T B Minshew Lt Col
Comm 1/6 R W R War R

OPERATION ORDER NO. 43 BY LIEUT. COLONEL F.E.DANIELSEN

COMMANDING 1/6 R.WAR.REGT.   Copy No........

October 11th, 1916.

Reference Map
1/20,000 57D N.E.

1. The 1/6 Bn. Royal Warwickshire Regiment will relive the 7th. Bn. Worcester Regiment placing B Coy. in the line from K 4 c 1 1 to K.3.d.3.6. – D Coy. in HEBUTERNE – Headquarters, A & C Coys in FONQUEVILLERS. Dress: Fighting Order.

2. B & D Coys. will parade at 8-0 a.m. and will march via SOUASTRE BAYENCOURT, SAILLY-AU-BOIS to J.24.b.8.5. then along valley road K.15.c.2.7. to HEBUTERNE. Platoon guides will be at HEBUTERNE POND at 10-0 a.m. After leaving BAYENCOURT, platoons will move at 200 yards distance.

3. Both Coys. cookers, carrying Officers mess boxes, will proceed in rear of Coys. The two Coys. blankets will be taken up at night.

4. A, C & Headquarters Coys will parade at 8-30 a.m. and will proceed via SOUASTRE and the Dummy Gun Route which runs J.4.b.7.3, J.5.a., D.29.c. & d, D.30.a., D.30.b.2.8., E.19.c. & d, E.20.c & d, enter FONQUEVILLERS along Cemetery Road. Marching in platoons at interval of 200 yards from J.4.b.7.3.

5. Cookers and transport with blankets for these two Coys. will proceed along SOUASTRE, FONQUEVILLERS Road. Platoon guides will be at Cemetery at FONQUEVILLERS at 10-0 a.m.

6. All blankets will be rolled (in tens) and collected at a central spot in each Coy. area ready for collection at 7-15 a.m. All packs should be delivered to R.S.M. at Billet 48 between 6-30 and 7-0 a.m.

7. Coys. will report to Battn. H.Qrs. FONQUEVILLERS immediately relief is complete.

8. Lewis Gun Handcarts. Two per Coy. will be taken up and should move with transport

9. Coy. Q.M.Sgts and Storemen will go up with Coys.

10. Separate Orders have been issued to the Transport Officer.

11. Water-bottles will be filled tonight.

S.E.Bowden 2/Lieut.

Issued by Orderly at 5-30 p.m.   A/Adjutant, 1/6 Bn. R.War.Regt.

Copy No. 1 Filed
2 War Diary
3 O.C. A Coy.
4 "   B "
5 "   C "
6 "   D "
7 7th. Worcester Regt.
8. Medical Officer.
9 Quartermaster.
10 Adjutant.

SECRET.

1/6 Royal Warwickshire Regt.

OPERATION ORDER NO 44.

Copy No 1

The Battalion will march with the Brigade to billets at GRAND RULLECOURT.

Coys. will form up in the following order:- "B", "C", "D" & "A", with the 3 Lewis Gun handcarts in rear of Coys. Head of column facing towards the Church opposite Brigade H.Q.Mess, ready to move at 2-10 p.m. Dress - full marching order, steel helmets to be worn. The Band will fall in at the head of the column.

Officers' valises to be at Battn. H.Q. Orderly Room yard at 12-0 noon. The mess cart will be at "B" Coys. mess at 1-0 p.m., and call at the other Coys. in turn, arriving at H.Q. at 1-30 p.m.

"A" Coy. will detail a rear party.

The Maltese cart will be at the Medical Inspection Room at 11-0 a.m.

Pioneers, shoemakers and Orderly Room boxes will be ready at 11-30 a.m.

The packs and rifles of the band will be carried by the Transport.

O.C.Coys are to hand to the Adjutant on falling in, a parade state also a certificate that all billets are left clean and tidy.

Pioneers, 2 sanitary men per Coy., and 2 H.Q.servants under 2/Lt Stephenson will remain behind to clear up.

(sd) S.E.BOWDEN, 2/Lt.
A/Adjt. 1/6th R.War.Regt.

20.10.1916.

War Diary.
File.
O.C.Coys. (4)
Transport Offr.
Adjt.

WAR DIARY or INTELLIGENCE SUMMARY

Army Form C. 2118.

1/6th R. War R   November 1916   Vol 21

Place	Date	Hour	Summary of Events and Information	Remarks and references to Appendices
ALBERT	1st		Marched to billets in ALBERT. Reinforcement 5 O.R.	J.D.M.
"	2nd		In billets	J.D.M.
FRICOURT	3rd		March to PEAKE WOOD CAMP. Casualties × 22 cordial	J.D.M.
"	4th		In Camp. Finding working parties	J.D.M.
"	5th		In Camp	J.D.M.
"	6th		In Camp	J.D.M.
"	7th		"	J.D.M.
"	8th		"	J.D.M.
MARTINPUICH	9th		Relieved 7th Yorcashis as right support battalion. Reinforcement 5 O.R.	J.D.M.
"	10th		In Support. Finding working parties. Casualties 1 O.R. wounded	J.D.M.
"	11th		" Casualties 1 O.R. wounded	J.D.M.
LE SARS	12th		Relieved 1/5th R War R in front line about 11 p.m. on 11th. Casualties 1 K.I.W.O.R.	J.D.M.
"	13th		In Front Trenches. Casualties 1 O.R. wounded. MAJ J R NUTTALL joined (14th)	J.D.M.
"	14th		" Capt R.S. PARTRIDGE wounded 7 O.R. wounded	J.D.M.
FRICOURT	15th		Relieved about 10 p.m. (14th) by 1/3rd Glos Regt – marched to SHELTER WOOD CAMP	J.D.M.
"	16		Rest in Camp. 1 O.R. wounded	J.D.M.
"	17		" Finding working parties. Reinforcement 7 O R	J.D.M.

Army Form C. 2118.

1/6th R War R

WAR DIARY
or
INTELLIGENCE SUMMARY. Nov 1916

(Erase heading not required.)

Instructions regarding War Diaries and Intelligence Summaries are contained in F. S. Regs., Part II. and the Staff Manual respectively. Title pages will be prepared in manuscript.

Place	Date	Hour	Summary of Events and Information	Remarks and references to Appendices
FRICOURT	18th		In Div Reserve - Finding working parties	J.L.M
"	19th		"	J.L.M
"	20th		"	J.L.M
"	21st		"	J.L.M
"	22nd		"	J.L.M
"	23rd		"	J.L.M
"	24th		"	J.L.M
MARTINPUICH	25th		2/Lt TONKING. 3rd OCLI - 2/Lt R.A.STEPHENSON 2/Lt C.J.MYERS. 2/Lt W.C. WILLIAMS 3/5th Essex Regt. transferred to 10th R War R. Relieved 1/8th Worcester Regt as left support Battalion - night 24th/25th - R & X Coy forward - A & Y Co + H Q in village - Reinforcement Capt. J.N. STAFFORD & 13 O.R. In Support.	J.L.M
"	26		Finding Working Parties. Casualties 1 O.R. killed 1 W	J.L.M
"	27		"	J.L.M
"	28		Relieve 1/5th R War R as centre battalion in line	J.L.M
LE SARS	29		In Trenches. Casualties O.R 1 K. 8 Wounded	J.L.M
"	30		"	J.L.M

7.12.16 Nicolas Lister
Commanding 1/6 R War R

CONFIDENTIAL.

War Diary of

1/6th Bn. Royal Warwickshire Regt.

From 1st December, 1916 to 31st December, 1916.

Army Form C. 2118.

WAR DIARY
or
INTELLIGENCE SUMMARY.

1/6 R.W.R.   Dec 1916

(Erase heading not required.)

Place	Date	Hour	Summary of Events and Information	Remarks and references to Appendices
LE SARS.	1st		In trenches. Reinforcement 9 O.R. 1 Wounded	J.d.h
"	2nd		In trenches. At 9.30 a.m. enemy raided a Lewis Gun Post - killing 2 men wounding 2 men - post was immediately counter attacked and regained by party under Sergt. WINDMILL. Casualties 2 K 4 W O.R.	J.d.h
CONTALMAISON	3rd		Relieved by 1/8th Worcester Regt. on evening of 2nd - Moved to Pioneer Camp Casualties 1 O.R Died	J.d.h
"	4		In Div. Reserve.	J.d.h
"	5		"	J.d.h
"	6		Found 3 working party	J.d.h
MARTINPUICH	7		Relieved 1/4th Glos Regt on evening of 6th as Left support Battalion	J.d.m
"	8		In Support. Reinforcement 7 O.R. m.g.	J.d.h
LE SARS	9		Relieved 1/5th R.W.R as centre front Battalion on evening of 8th - Raid which was to take place in early hours of 9th postponed until 6-30 p.m. result capture of 4 O.R. of 1st Batt 2nd Marine Div. - 2 O.R. severe. Party Capt R S Partridge - 2/Lt Gosse and 23 O.R. Casualties 1 O.R. wounded	J.d.h
"	10		In Trenches Casualties 3 K 4 W O.R	J.d.h
CONTALMAISON	11		Relieved by 1/4th Glos. Regt on evening of 10th	J.d.h

1577 Wt.W10791/1773 500,000 1/15 D.D.&L. A.D.S.S./Form/C. 2118.

WAR DIARY
INTELLIGENCE SUMMARY.

1/6th R War R

Army Form C. 2118.

Place	Date	Hour	Summary of Events and Information	Remarks and references to Appendices
CONTALMAISON	November 12		During November Military Medals awarded to No 1495 CoSM DAWE (Killed) No 2624 Cpl L BARDELL. No 2759 Cpl T.E. BEASTALL. No 1374 Pte D A COATES. No 2672 Cpl H W DAVIES. No 338 Sgt W HIGGS. No 230 C.Q.M.S A SMITH. No 1266 Sgt H SMITH.	J.L.M
"	13		In Divl. Reserve. Major W.M. PRYOR 1/Hertfordshire Regt. joined for duty	J.L.M
BECOURT	14		Relieved by 10th Scottish Rifles - marched to BECOURT. M.M. awarded to No 2799 Sgt. C. WINDMILL	J.L.M
MILLENCOURT	15		marched to MILLENCOURT camp	J.L.M
"	16		Rest.	J.L.M
"	17		Training	J.L.M
"	18		"	J.L.M
"	19		" Reinforcement 9 O.R.	J.L.M
"	20		" " 1 O.R.	J.L.M
"	21		"	J.L.M
"	22		" " 3 O.R	J.L.M
"	23		" M C awarded to Capt. R.S. PARTRIDGE	J.L.M
"	24		" " 6 O.R	J.L.M
"	25		"	J.L.M

Army Form C. 2118.

WAR DIARY
or
INTELLIGENCE SUMMARY.

December 1/6" R 45an R.

(Erase heading not required.)

Place	Date	Hour	Summary of Events and Information	Remarks and references to Appendices
MILLENCOURT	26		Training	Appx
	27		"	Appx
	28		Marched to harbour	Appx
	29		Training	Appx
	30		"	Appx
	31		"	Appx

Reinforcements 9 O.R.

windup of 1/6 R Warwickshire
comd. 1/6 R Warwickshire

OPERATION ORDER No. 45 BY LIEUT. COLONEL F.G. DANIELSEN, COMMDG.
1/6TH R. WAR. REGT.   Copy No. ....

November 9th, 1916.

1. The 1/6th Royal Warwickshire Regiment will relieve the support Battalion of the right sector of the Brigade front this evening.

2. The Battalion will parade ready to move off at 3.30 p.m. Dress: New order of fighting kit with leather jerkins rolled inside oil sheet. Order of march will be "B","D","A","C".

3. Packs and overcoats will be dumped at PEAKE WOOD STATION by 10.30 a.m.

4. The route will be via Northern End of MAMETZ WOOD and BAZENTIN JUNCTION.

5. Platoons will march with 200 yards distance. Platoon guides and one guide for Battalion Headquarters from 7th Worcester Regt. will meet the Battalion at BAZENTIN JUNCTION at 5.0 p.m.

6. The rations carried will be unexpended portion of rations for 9th inst. and the whole of the rations for consumption on 10th inst.

7. Lewis Guns and ammunition will be carried on pack ponies, parading at 2.0 p.m. Each Coy's pack pony will march behind its leading platoon.

8. Water bottles will be filled before marching off.

9. Company Commanders are held responsible that the men rub their feet with anti-frostbite grease before parading.

                                        Snowden 2/Lt.
                               A/Adjt. 1/6th R. War. Regt.

Copy No 1 Filed.
     2 War Diary.
     3 O.C. A Coy.
     4 O.C. B Coy.
     5 O.C. C Coy.
     6 O.C. D Coy.
     7 Adjutant.

Ref: Map

1/40,0000 ALBERT COMBINED SHEET.
1/10,000 LE SARS SHEET.
1/10,000 48 Div SECRET Map Edn.1.

OPERATION ORDER NO 46 BY LIEUT. COL. F.G. DANIELSEN,
Comm 1/6 R.WAR.Regt.

Copy No.....

Dcr 5/1916

1. The 1/6 R.War.Regt. will relieve the left support battn., the 4th. Gloucester Regt., tomorrow.

2. The first platoon will march off at 3-30 p.m.

3. Dress; Fighting Order over greatcoats. A spare pair of socks must be carried in the haversack.

4. Order of march, C, B, D Coys., Headquarters, A Coy., Working Company.

5. All packs and blankets (securely rolled in bundles of 10 and labelled clearly) must be ready for removal to store by 11-0 a.m.

6. The Battalion will march via Villa Station and Corduroy Track. Guides will be at West End Dump. Platoons will march at 200 yards distance.

7. Rations carried will be the unexpended portion for the 6th. and rations for the 7th.

8. Lewis Guns, Magazines etc will proceed by limber at 2-0 p.m. and will be picked up at the same spot as last relief. One man per Company will be ready to proceed with the limber

9. Coy. Commanders are warned to be sure that every man's feet have been rubbed with whale oil; that they have breech and muzzle covers on the rifles; that their gas helmets have have been inspected during the morning by the Company Gas N.C.O. and that water-bottles are full when marching off.

10. The Transport Officer will report at the Orderly Room at 8-30 a.m. tomorrow for orders.

11. Gum Boots and Waterproof Capes. Equal numbers of each will be drawn from the Corporal of the Guard by B, D and C Coys between 11-0 a.m. and Noon tomorrow.

12. Completion of relief must be reported to Battalion H.Qs. at once.

Captain,
A/Adjutant, 1/6 R.War.R

Issued by orderly at 8-0 p.m.

No. 1 File.
    2 War Diary.
    3. O.C. A Coy.
    4. "   B "
    5. "   C "
    6. "   D "
    7. Q.M. and T.O.
    8. Spare.

Operation Order No 47
by
Lt. Col. F G Danielsen   No 1
commanding 1/6th R.War.R.

1. A party of the battalion will carry out a raid.

2. Object to raid copse at M 10 d 1.2 to inflict casualties & capture prisoners

3. Composition - Storming party 2/Lieut GOSSE - 1 Sergt & 13 O.R - Covering party Capt. R.S. PARTRIDGE & 7 men.

4. The party will depart & return from Scotland Trench at M 16 a. 8. 8.

5. The party will not leave our trenches before midnight.

6. Orders have been issued for Artillery fire when the party returns if called upon by a red very light signal.

J L Mellor / Capt &
a/Adj
1/6th R War R

Dec. 8th/16
No 1 War Diary
No 2 File
3 to 5. Issued

OPERATION ORDER NO 48, BY LT. COL. F¥G¥DANIELSEN, COMMDG.

1/6TH R. WAR. REGT.

Copy No........

Dec. 13th 1916.

1.   The Battalion will be relieved in Divnl. Res. by the 10th Scottish Rifles, and will proceed to BECOURT tomorrow.

2.   The Battalion will be ready to move off at 9.50 a.m. Coys. falling in, in front of their own lines and Headquarters in front of Officers' huts.

3.   They will move off at 9.50 a.m. with 100 yards intervals between platoons.

4.   Dress: Full marching order.

5.   An unloading place has been pointed out to the Orderly N.C.O. of each Company by the R.S.M. Coys. are responsible that all blankets are stacked there, carefully rolled and tallied in tens, also all Officers' valises, by 9.0 a.m.

6.   1 N.C.O. and 20 men from each of "A" & "B" Coys. will report to the R.S.M. at the Orderly Room at 8.0 a.m. to take Gum Boots and other stores to the same point, and 1 N.C.O. and 10 men from each of "C" & "D" Coys. will report at Headquarters Mess at the same hour.

7.   All braziers should be stacked in the guard room before 9.0 a.m.

8.   2/Lt. J. Harrison and 1 junior N.C.O. from each Coy. will hand over to incoming unit.

9.   2/Lt G.H.L. Easterbrook and C.Q.M. Sergts. will act as advance party, leaving the Orderly Room at 8.30 a.m., and report to the Town Major, BECOURT at 9.30 a.m.

10. Company Commanders and 2/Lt. J. Rhodes (for the 5 Headquarters huts) will hand a certificate to the Adjutant at 9.30 a.m. that the huts in their area are left in a clean and tidy condition.

11. Mess boxes, pioneers, shoemakers and Orderly Room boxes will be stacked on the footboards between the Orderly Room and the Guard Room before 8.30 a.m.

J.J. Mellor
Capt.

A/Adjt. 1/6th R. War. Regt.

Issued by orderly at

No 1. File.
 2. War Diary.
 3. O.C. "A" Coy.
 4. O.C. "B" Coy.
 5. O.C. "C" Coy.
 6. O.C. "D" Coy.
 7. Adjutant.

OPERATION ORDER NO 49, BY LT. COL. F.G. DANIELSEN, COMDG.

1/6TH R. WAR. REGT.

14.12.1916.

Copy No ....

1. The Battalion will march to MILLENCOURT on the morning of the 15th Dec.

2. Dress: Full marching order, steel helmets.

3. The Battalion will parade ready to move off at 10.0 a.m. Order of march, Headquarters, "B" & "C" Coys., Band, "D" & "A" Coys. Coys. will proceed with 100 yards interval between platoons.

4. Lt. Seel, four C.Q.M.Sergts. and Sergt. Smith (Headquarters) will leave the Orderly Room at 8.15 a.m. to report to the Staff Captain at Millencourt at 10.30 a.m. as billetting party.

5. 2/Lt. Belcher, six men per gun, and one N.C.O. per Coy. (taking into consideration the guard) will leave the Camp at 8.30 a.m. proceeding across country to where the guns are parked and march independently via ALBERT to MILLENCOURT.

6. 2/Lt. Easterbrook and one junior N.C.O. from each Coy. will hand over Camp and give necessary certificates to Town Major.

7. All blankets, gum boots, baggage etc. will be loaded in the same place as unloaded today, before 8.30 a.m.

8. Part transport will proceed with column, the remainder joining in Albert.

9. Marching State and Clean Billets Certificate will be handed to the Adjutant at the Orderly Room by 9.30 a.m.

10. Lorries etc. will be here by 8.30 a.m.

Capt.

A/Adjt. 1/6th R. War.Regt.

No 1. War Diary.
2. File.
3. O.C. "A" Coy.
4. O.C. "B" Coy.
5. O.C. "C" Coy.
6. O.C. "D" Coy.
7. T.O.
8. Adjutant.

OPERATION ORDER NO 59 BY MAJOR E.E.PRYOR, COMDG. 1/6th R. WAR. REGT.

Copy No................

Dec. 27th 1916.

1. The Battalion will march to WARLOY on the morning of December 28th.

2. Dress: Full marching order, steel helmets to be carried on packs.

3. The Battalion will parade ready to move off at 10.20 a.m. Order of march, Headquarters, Band, "A", "B", "C" & "D" Coys. Companies will proceed with 100 yards interval between platoons.

4. 2/Lt. T. Ruddock and four C.Q.M.Sergts. and Sergt. Smith (Headquarters) will report to the Town Major at Warloy 9.30 a.m. as a billeting party.

5. 2/Lt. Draper and one junior N.C.O. from each Coy. will hand over the Camp to the Town Major, giving the necessary certificates.

6. All blankets will be rolled in bundles of ten and plainly marked. Gum boots, blankets, packages etc. will be stacked on the road by the Orderly Room before 9.0 a.m.
    Officers' valises and Coy. mess boxes are to be ready to be loaded at 9.30 a.m.

7. The Transport will follow the Battalion 100 yards between sections.

8. Marching State and Clean Billets Certificate will be handed to the Adjutant at the Orderly Room at 10.0 a.m.

                                           Lieut.

                      A/Adjt. 1/6th R. War. Regt.

No 1. War Diary.
    2. File.
    3. O.C. "A" Coy.
    4. O.C. "B" Coy.
    5. O.C. "C" Coy.
    6. O.C. "D" Coy.
    7. T.O.
    8. Adjutant.

Confidential

War Diary

1/6° R. Warwickshire Regt.

1st Jan. 1917 —— 31st Jan. 1917

Army Form C. 2118.

1/6th Royal Warwickshire Rgt.

WAR DIARY
or
INTELLIGENCE SUMMARY.

January 1917

(Erase heading not required.)

Instructions regarding War Diaries and Intelligence Summaries are contained in F. S. Regs., Part II. and the Staff Manual respectively. Title pages will be prepared in manuscript.

Place	Date	Hour	Summary of Events and Information	Remarks and references to Appendices
WARLOY	1		Training	
"	2		Major J. R. Nuttall left for ENGLAND	
"	3		Reinforcements 203 o.R.	
"	4		Reinforcements 21 o.R.	
"	5		"	
"	6		"	
"	7		"	
"	8		Batt. marched to MERICOURT L'ABBÉ, by train to AIRAINES, marched to LIERCOURT.	
LIERCOURT	9		Resting. 2Lt A.T. Browning, 3/6 R. WAR R., joined for duty.	
"	10		Training. Reinforcements 10 o.R.	
"	11		"	
"	12		"	
"	13		"	
"	14		"	
"	15		Reinforcements 1 o.R.	
"	16		2Lt J. Ruddock to ENGLAND, sick	
"	17		"	
"	18		Reinforcements 3 o.R.	
"	19		Reinforcements 3 o.R. Lt & QM. M. A. Jindler left for ENGLAND.	
"	20		2Lt W. S. Gahee to R.F.C.	
"	21			
"	22			
"	23		Reinforcements 6 o.R.	
"	24		Reinforcements 1 o.R.	
"	25			
"	26			
"	27		Batt. marched to PONT REMY, by train to CERISY, marched to MERICOURT SUR SOMME	
MERICOURT	28		Training	
"	29		Reinforcements 2 o.R.	
"	30		"	
"	31		Batt. marched to CAPPY.	

OPERATION ORDER NO 51 BY MAJOR W.M.PRYOR, COMMDG. 1/6TH R.WAR.REGT.

Copy No.........

6/1/1917

1. The Battalion will move to new training area on Monday, 8th inst. Transport and cookers will leave on the morning of the 7th.

2. Three motor lorries for blankets and Coy. Mess Boxes, Officers' kits, and Orderly Room boxes will be at the church at 7.0 a.m. on the 9th. Time for dumping the above will be notified later.

3. Each man will carry one blanket, remainder to be rolled and tied in bundles of 10 and clearly marked.

4. Pioneers and shoemakers' stores will be loaded on Transport tonight.

5. Lewis Guns in their handcarts will be taken on the train. Tin ammunition boxes that cannot be put in handcarts will be loaded on the Transport tonight.

6. Cooking arrangements. Coys will keep back sufficient dixies for cooking purposes which will be loaded on lorries.

7. No baggage will be taken on the train.

8. Further orders as to time of starting etc. will be issued later.

9. After tonight the water for drinking purposes and for Officers Mess will be drawn from Headquarters. Water for cooking purposes will be drawn from water point near Transport lines.

10. Each Coy. will detail one man to load up kits, blankets etc. and go with lorries.

(sd) C.H.B.Seel, Lieut.
A/Adjt. 1/6th R. War. Regt.

1. File.
2. War Diary.
3. O.C. A.Coy.
4. "   B.Coy.
5. "   C.Coy.
6. "   D.Coy.
7. T.O.
8. Lewis Gun Officer.
9. Adjutant.

SUPPLIMENTARY TO OPERATION ORDER NO 51 BY MAJOR W.M.PRYOR,

COMMDG. 1/6TH R. WAR. REGT.

7/1/1916.

1. Battalion will parade at 12.0 noon in full marching order, with the blanket rolled in oilsheet and strapped on top of valise, and steel helmets in valise straps.

2. Battalion will fall in in the following order in the Rue D'Harpenville Signallers, Band, A. B. C. & D. Coys. Signallers on the right and D. Coy. on the left, and will move off at 100 yards between platoons. Remainder of details will parade with Coys.

3. Rolls containing the 2nd blanket will be dumped in the gateways of billets at 7.30 a.m. Officers' kits, mess boxes, dixies etc. to be dumped at quartermaster's stores at 9.0 a.m.

4. Sufficient rations for the day to be carried on the man, water bottles to be filled tonight.

5. Billeting party consisting of 2/Lt. Alsop, C.Q.M.Sergts. and Sergt. Smith, will report to Adjutant for orders on detraining.

6. O.C.Coys. will render a certificate to the Adjutant at 11.45 a.m. that all their billets have been left in a clean and tidy condition, and a return showing the exact number of Officers and Other Ranks on parade at 12 noon. The acting R.S.M. will render these returns for Headquarters Coy.

(sd) C.H.B.Seal, Lieut.
A/Adjt. 1/6th R. War. Regt.

OPERATION ORDER NO 53 BY LT. COL. F.C.DANIELSEN, D.S.O.

COMMDG. 1/6TH R. WAR. REGT.

Copy No........

26/1/1917.

1. The Battalion will parade ready to move off at 7.30 a.m. tomorrow as follows:- Drums, A. & D. Coys. outside Battalion Headquarters. - B. & C. Coys. on the main PONT-REMY ROAD with the rear of the column at the junction of the road leading to Battalion Headquarters. All details (except Drums) will parade with Coys.

2. Lewis Gun Handcarts will follow in rear of Coys.

3. Loading of Lewis Gun Handcarts. On arrival at station the bodies of handcarts will be removed from wheels ready to load.

4. 2/Lt. F.B.Williams will act as entraining and detraining Officer. He will report to the R.T.O. PONT-REMY at 7.30 a.m. Marching out state will be handed to him at C. Coys.Headquarters at 7.0 a.m. without fail.

5. Dress - Full Marching Order, wearing steel hats and greatcoats. Each man will carry one blanket.

6. Remainder of blankets, in bundles of ten and securely tied and plainly marked, will be stacked in Headquarters yard at 6.15 a.m. Officers' kits and mess boxes will be dumped at same place by 7.0 a.m. All other stores to be at Headquarters at 6.30 a.m.

7. B. Coy. will provide one platoon as loading party, to be at PONT-REMY Station at 7.15 a.m. with all their kit. They will pile arms and dump equipment and report to 2/Lt. Williams on his arrival at 7.30 a.m. The same Coy. will detail another platoon to be at Battalion Headquarters to load lorries at 6.30 a.m. On arrival at CERISY both platoons will again form loading party from the train to the lorries. The remaining two platoons of B. Coy. will push on to MERRICOURT-SUR-SOMME and act as unloading party there.

8. O.C.Coys. will inspect billets and before the Battalion moves off, and hand to Orderly Room a certificate that billets are left clean and that Officers Messes have been paid for.

(sd) C.H.B.Soel, Lieut.
A/Adjt. 1/6th R. War. Regt.

Issued at 7.30 p.m.

1. File.   5 - C Coys.
2. War Diary.   6.   Adjt.

CONFIDENTIAL.

WAR DIARY of

1/6th Bn. R. WARWICKSHIRE REGT.

From 1st FEB. TO 28th FEB. 1917.

****

Army Form C. 2118.

WAR DIARY
or
INTELLIGENCE SUMMARY.

February 17th 1/6th R War R

(Erase heading not required.)

Instructions regarding War Diaries and Intelligence Summaries are contained in F. S. Regs., Part II. and the Staff Manual respectively. Title pages will be prepared in manuscript.

Place	Date	Hour	Summary of Events and Information	Remarks and references to Appendices
CAPPY	1/2		Battalion took over line south of BIACHES – 3 companies in line – one company left at ECLUSIER as working company – Relieved 2/25th Reg d'Infantry	J.L.M
BIACHES	2/2		In Trenches. Casualties 3 O.R wounded	J.L.M
"	3/2		" " 5 O.R "	J.L.M
"	4/2		Heavily bombarded between 12 (noon) and 5-40 p.m with three separate lulls – intense bombardment 5-40 – Barrage on Front Support & STETTIN lines and Communication Trenches – Raiding parties entered left of centre company (B.Co) at 6.15 p.m – other parties on right and left stopped by L.G and rifle fire. – S.O.S signals sent up 6.15. and H.Q communicated with Brigade on telephone just as lines were cut – centre and left companies moved up supports – found enemy already driven out at 6.25 p.m. Casualties. 2/Lt F.J.T. BELCHER killed – O.R 3 Killed. 4 Died of Wounds. 65 Wounded. 14 missing. Apprvd by 1st Prussian Guard.	J.L.M
"	5/2		Relieved by 1/5th R War R. Moved into Div. Reserve at Camp 58. Reinforcement. 10 O.R	J.L.M
"	6/2		In Div. Res. Training	J.L.M
"	7/2		" "	J.L.M
"	8/2		" "	J.L.M
"	9/2		" "	J.L.M

February 1917 WAR DIARY 1/6 R War R
or
INTELLIGENCE SUMMARY.

Army Form C. 2118.

(Erase heading not required.)

Hour, Date, Place	Summary of Events and Information	Remarks and references to Appendices
ECOUST Feb.	Immediate rewards for action of Feb 4th	
	Capt. R.A. KERR. R.A.M.C attached M.C	
	2/Lt. F.B. WILLIAMS M.C	
	2/Lt. J. HARRISON M.C	
	No 20343 C.S.M BILLINGTON. F.W D.C.M	
	20839 Corp. McKAY E.J. D.C.M	
	55763 Pt. WOSKETT. T.A. M.M	
	20253 Pt. EXLEY. C.H. M.M	
	1952 Pt BENZING. T. M.M	
	2698 Sergt. CHANNING W. M.M	
	1531 L/Cpl BAYLISS. A.E M.M	
	2624 Sergt. BARDELL L. Bar to M.M.	

Army Form C. 2118.

February 1917 WAR DIARY 1/6th R.War.R
or
INTELLIGENCE SUMMARY.

(Erase heading not required.)

Instructions regarding War Diaries and Intelligence Summaries are contained in F.S. Regs., Part II. and the Staff Manual respectively. Title pages will be prepared in manuscript.

Hour, Date, Place		Summary of Events and Information	Remarks and references to Appendices
BIACHE	Feb 10	Relieved 1/5th R.War.R in Trenches	J.2.h
"	11	In Trenches Casualties 1 O.R. K. 9. O.R W both accidentally	J.2.h
"	12	" Casualties, O.R.W. Reinforcement 1 O.R	J.2.h
"	13	"	J.2.h
WILLKINO	" 14	Relieved by 1/5th R.War.R - moved into Brigade Reserve in WILLKINO Huts	J.2.h
"	15	In Bg. Reserve Lt. E. Spencer joined for duty.	J.2.h
"	16	"	J.2.h
"	17	" 1 O.R. W. accidentally	J.2.h
"	18	"	J.2.h
"	19	"	J.2.h
BIACHE	20	Relieved 1/5th R.War.R in Trenches	J.2.h
"	21	In Trenches 2/Lt. B.F. DOWSETT joined for duty.	J.2.h
"	22	" 8.30 p.m. Front heavily bombarded 7.40 p.m to 8 p.m Casualties O.R. 1 Killed, 15 O.R.W.	J.2.h
"	23	" Front again bombarded at 5.45 a.m Casualties O.R. 1 Killed, 1 W.	J.2.h
"	24	Reinforcement 7 O.R Casualties 1 O.R. wounded	J.2.h

February 1917 WAR DIARY or INTELLIGENCE SUMMARY. 1/5' R.War.R

Army Form C. 2118.

(Erase heading not required.)

Hour, Date, Place	Summary of Events and Information	Remarks and references to Appendices
BIACHE Feb 26.	In Trenches. Rumour enemy were evacuating but three patrols found posts occupied.	JdM

ECLUSIER 26	Relieved by 1/5th R.War.R. Sent out patrol to secure an identification - not successful - 2/25 DRAPER seriously wounded. Moved into Bn Reserve. The undermentioned honours and awards were bestowed among the New Year awards:-
	
	 G.S.O. Lt-Col F.G. DANIELSEN
	 M.C. Lt. J. WALKER (attached 143 Inf Bde)
	         Capt. J.L. MELLOR.
	         2/Lieut J.G. COOPER
	
	 Specially 1732 C.S.M. Y. WALDRON (KILLED)
	 mentioned 2817 Sgt. P.N GIBBS
	 in Dispatches 2086 Y a/Cpl. C. ETHERIDGE
	              2021 a/L/Cpl W. BROOKS.
		JdM

ECLUSIER 27	In Bn Reserve. Resting & Bathing	JdM
" 28	" "	JdM

OPERATION ORDER NO ?? BY LT. COL. F.G. DANIELSEN, D.S.O., COMDG.
1/6TH R. WAR. REGT.

No............
10/4/17.

Reference Maps. Sheet. 62c N. 1/20000.
               PERONNE. 1/10000.

1. The Battalion will relieve 1/8th Bn. Royal Warwickshire Regt. tonight.

2. The Brigade frontage has been changed and the right boundry is exclusive. The Southern boundary of the Battalion will be DOLLFUS to Junction of STETTIN inclusive,- thence along STETTIN to ROYAU BURGER exclusive. The North boundary to be decided.

3. The Battalion will move off at 4.0 p.m. with 300 yards between platoons, in the following order - C. D. H.Q. & B.

4. Dress - Fighting order, wearing great coats with one blanket. No puttees are to be worn, but are to be packed in valise. Sand bags to be drawn.

5. A. Coy. will remain Working Company and take over exact dispositions of last tour, arranging their own billeting party.

6. Dispositions in the line - D. Coy. on the right - C. Coy. on the left - B. Coy. in support.

7. Guides will be on the sunken road near old Brigade Headquarters at 6.30 p.m.

8. The Battalion Headquarters will be in IGLAU. Brigade Headquarters at N.?2.d.6.6.

9. Tea will be served near Herbecourt at the 4.15 halt.

10. All Working Companies going up from the rear will take their arms with them as far as the Dump. They may be piled there, left under a guard and picked up on the return of the party.

11. Carrying parties etc., by night, will always proceed above ground in order to permit trenches to be kept in proper repair. A path for each Battn. must be reconnoitred and marked.

12. Movement during Day time is to be reduced to a minimum, and no men are to be out of trenches forward of Bde. Hdqrs.

13. A carrying party of 25 men from A.Coy. together with one servant per Coy. will parade outside Orderly Room at 3.30 p.m. to accompany limber carrying Headquarters & Coy. Mess boxes and Medical Stores.

14. Valises and mess boxes to be stacked behind C.Coy. Hut at 3.30 p.m. and Blanket and packs to be stacked at the end of each Coy. hut at 2.55 p.m.
C.Q.M.Stores, Shoemakers, Pioneers & Orderly Room boxes to be at Coy. Q.M.Stores hut at 2.30 p.m.

15. Coy. will detail ration party tonight.

(sd) J.L.MELLOR, Capt.
A/Adjt. 1/6th R. War. Regt.

1 File.
2 War Diary.
3 - 6 O.C.Coys.
7 Adjutant.

1/1 25

25
(9 sheets)

Confidential.

War Diary of

1/6" Bn R. Warwickshire R.

1st to 31st March 1917

WAR DIARY 1/6th R. War R.
or
INTELLIGENCE SUMMARY.

Army Form C. 2118.

March 1917

(Erase heading not required.)

Hour, Date, Place	Summary of Events and Information	Remarks and references to Appendices
ECLUSIER Mar 1	In Bn Reserve – Camp 56.	J.d.m.
" 2	" Casualties 2 Wounded on Working Party	J.d.m.
" 3	"	J.d.m.
" 4	"	J.d.m.
" 5	" Casualties 1 O.R. died	J.d.m.
" 6	"	J.d.m.
" 7	" Reinforcements 8 O.R.	J.d.m.
" 8	Relieved 1/8th Worcesters in old section – right of 1/8th. Raid carried out by A Co at 9 p.m. Bombarded by trench mortars for 10 minutes before zero – Barrage from zero to +10 then forming a box – party in trenches 15 mins – 3 Prisoners (one died) & one machine gun – estimate over 30 Germans killed. Casualties O.R. 1 Killed 2 Wounded & Missing – 13 Wounded (one remained at duty) 3 in trenches. Casualties O.R. 3 K. 5 W.	J.d.m.
9	Reinforcement 1 O.R.	J.d.m.
10	"	J.d.m.
BIACHE 11	" Casualties O.R. 2 K. 1 W	J.d.m.
12	" 2/Lt J.W. BISSEKER joined	J.d.m.

Army Form C. 2118.

March 1917.   1/6' R W Fan R

WAR DIARY
or
INTELLIGENCE SUMMARY.
(Erase heading not required.)

Hour, Date, Place		Summary of Events and Information	Remarks and references to Appendices
BIACHE	Mar 13	In Trenches. Corp. R H Dane graded M M.	J.L.m
ECLUSIER	" 14	Relieved by 1/5'R W Fan R on night 13/14 March	J.L.m
	15	Moved into Brigade Reserve (Camp 50 Bns.) Battery etc	J.L.m
	16	Reinforcement 1 O.R.	J.L.m
	17	Enemy's trenches opposite Brigade sector evacuated	J.L.m
MEREAUCOURT WOOD	18	Moved forward. H Q & 2 Coys to WOOD. C Co to HERBECOURT. D. Co to MITTIAN D. 1/6' R War R entered PERONNE	J.L.m
	19	Working Parties. M M granted to 5743. Pte. W G. DAVIES 20743. Pte W C SMITH. 20855. Pte C DOODY Casualties 1 O R accidentally wounded	J.L.m
	20	"	J.L.m
	21	"	J.L.m
	22	"	J.L.m
	23	"	J.L.m
	24	"	J.L.m

Army Form C. 2118.

WAR DIARY
or
INTELLIGENCE SUMMARY.
(Erase heading not required.)

March 1917 1/6th R War R

Hour, Date, Place		Summary of Events and Information	Remarks and references to Appendices
PERONNE	Mar 25	Battalion moved to billets in PERONNE (24th) Capt J A FYSHE & 2/Lt A V BETTS joined for duty. Working Parties	J.I.M
	26	In Reserve	J.I.M
BUSSU	27	Moved to BUSSU. HQ & 2 Coys at BUSSU. Reinforcement 15 OR	J.I.M
SAULCOURT	28	2 Coys to AIZECOURT le Haut. Relieved 1/4th R War R in outpost line in front of SAULCOURT. One company in line – one in support. Batt H Q & 2 Coys in GREBAUSSART WOOD.	J.I.M
GREBAUSSART	29	Relieved in outpost line by 1/6th Glou. Regt. – into companies to LONGAVESNES. Casualties 2 O R wounded	J.I.M
	30	In Reserve. ST EMILIE on night. HEUDECOURT on left captured	J.I.M
	31	In reserve	J.I.M

T/2nd/Lieut J W Bowyer taken prisoner
crossing 1/6 River R

OPERATION ORDER NO 56 BY LT. COL. F.G.DANIELSEN, D.S.O., COMMDG.
1/6TH R. WAR. REGT.

Ref. Sheet 62c.N.W. Ed 4, 1/10,000.   No............
PERONNE.
                                                6/3/17.

1. The 1/6th Bn. R.War.Regt. will relieve two Coys. of the 8th Bn. Worcester Regt. on the night of the 7/8th March 1917.

2. Dispositions of Coys: C. Coy. in front line, B. Coy. in IGLAU, A. Coy. in HERBECOURT & D. Coy. in WITTIKIND.

3. Guides for front two Coys. will be at WARWICK DUMP, H.29.d.68 at 7.0 p.m. and for HERBECOURT Coy. at West End of HERBECOURT at 6.15 p.m.

4. Coys. will move off in the following order:- C. Coy. 4.15 p.m. followed by B, H.Qrs., & A. Coy. An interval of 100 yards will be maintained between platoons.

5. Dress - Winter Fighting Order (with greatcoats).

6. All blankets will be returned to Q.M.Stores at undermentioned times, rolled in tens and need not be labelled.
    A. Coy. 11.0 a.m.   D. Coy. 12.30 p.m.
    B. Coy. 11.30 a.m.   H.Qrs. 1.0 p.m.
    C. Coy. 12.0 noon.

7. O.C.Coys. will report immediately relief is complete. A. & D. Coys. will send guides to remain at Headquarters.

8. Coys. will also send before 7.0 a.m. on 8th inst. a complete list of all stores and ammunition taken over.

9. O.C.Coys. & T.O. will attend at H.Qrs.Mess at 10.0 a.m. 7th inst. respecting further details.

                    (sd) J.L.MELLOR. Capt.
                    A/Adjt. 1/6th R. War. Regt.

File.
War Diary.
O.C.Coys.
Adjt.
T.O.

OPERATION ORDER NO. 58 BY LT.COL. P.G.DANIELSEN, D.S.O.   Copy No. 2.
              Commdg 1/6 R.WAR.REGT.   March 28th.1917.

Reference Sheet
62c N.E. 1/40,000.

1. The 1/6 R.War.Regt will take over the left Sector of the 143rd.
   Inf. Bde Outpost Line on the afternoon of the 28th.March 1917.

2. The line is along the road from E.25.a.26 through E.16.D.b & a.
   and thence along eastern edge of SAULCORT. The right boundary
   will be GRIBAUSSART WOOD, JEAN COPSE and E.16 Central. All
   inclusive to this Battalion.

3. Patrols are to be advanced to CAPRON COPSE, CHAUFOURS WOOD.

4. Companies will be distributed as follows: B Coy.Left front;
   C Coy. Right front; D Coy. Support and A Coy. Reserve.

5. C & D Coy. will move off at 1.30 pm. and A & B Coys at 2.0 pm.
   Parties to move in file with 200 yards between platoons.
   Headquarters will move behind B Company.

6. The Route is to be BRIERCOURT-TEMPLEUX-LAFOSSE-LARGAVESNES.

7. Dress: Fighting Order with greatcoats.

8. Half a limber will be allotted to A & D Coys to be accompanied
   by one servant and one Lewis Gunner from each Company and the
   same for B & C Coys. These limbers will move as far as possible
   behind the rear platoon of the leading Coy. and when unloaded by
   them will join their rear Coy.

9. Cookers will move in rear of their Coys. and be placed in rear
   a selected screened position by the Coy. Commander.

10. All packs (with blanket inside), Officers valises and mess
    boxes will be stacked in convenient places on road in front
    of Coy. H.Qrs. and will be left in charge of C.Q.M.Sergts
    who will not return to PERONNE until they have seen the whole
    of them loaded. Batmen will accompany Companies.

11. Limber for H.Qs., Tool Cart, S.A.A.Cart, Water Carts and
    Pack Ponies will move in rear of H.Qrs. Coy under the
    Transport Officer.

12. In case of attack by hostile aeroplanes, Officers and
    Platoon Comdrs. are to scatter their commands off the road.

                                      J.A. Shelby
                                                Captain,
Issued by Orderly at 10-15 am.   Adjutant, 1/6 R.War.Regt.

    Copy No. 1. File   Copy No. 8. Transport Officer.
      "   " 2 War Diary.   "   " 9 Adjutant,
      " 3 to 7 Companies.   "   " 10 Spare.

"Operation Order No 54"
by
Lt Col F G Danielsen D.S.O
Commanding 1/6th R War R.

Ref Map
1/5000 from Air Photo

1. A Co will make a raid on evening of 8th

2. Object to secure an identification cause loss to enemy & penetrate his second line

3. Following parties:- No 1 1 Off & 27 O.R
No 2 1 NCO & 20 O.R   No 3 1 NCO & 20 O.R.   No 4 1 Off & 20 O.R
Covering 1 Off & 20 O.R

4. The parties will assemble in front line between I 31 d 30.70 & I 31 d 30.95 and go out by Posts 4. 5 & 6

5. Party I will block front trench south of Pt 78 - deal with dugouts and C.T. running from Pt 78.
Party II enter same place and work N.N.E to C.T. from Pt 79 & along front line

5. Party III enters at Pt 79 and works due E along C T

Party IV enters at Pt 70. block to N and E and work S.S.E to C T running from Pt 79.8 along front line.

When party I reaches German second line they will work 50 yds N & S of point of entry

Covering party extended 50 yds from German front line

6. Artillery barrages have been arranged also M G & Stokes programmes

7. Telephone communication from covering party with whom is F O O — visual from STETTIN Co H Q

8. The party remain in 15 to 20 mins. Signal for withdrawal — Firing Red Very light & blowing of whistles

9. Medical Arrangements. 4 S B s with covering party — 4 in front line near Post 6. M O & 3 R A M C bearer parties in STETTIN

10. All prisoners to be sent at once under escort to Batt. HQ

Parties will return as far as possible to head of AUBERT

12. The hour of Zero will be 9 p.m. Artillery barrage will lift to form pocket at + 10.

2 p.m.
8.3.17

J L Mellor/ Capt & O/C
1/6' R War R

Army Form C. 2118.

April 1917 1/6' R War R

WAR DIARY or INTELLIGENCE SUMMARY.

(Erase heading not required.)

Vol 26

Hour, Date, Place		Summary of Events and Information	Remarks and references to Appendices
SAULCOURT	1/4	The Battalion took part in an attack by 143 & 144 Infy. Bde. on EPEHY and PEIZIERE - The battalion attacked and was supported by 1/5th R War R - B Co & C Co on left - A Co in reserve. Attack commenced at dawn. Its whole objective was secured by 6-40 a.m. Casualties 2/Lt J W BISSEKER killed. OR 9 K. 2 S of W. 25 W. 2/Lt R B W GOSSE died of wounds 2/Lt G H L Eastbrook wounded Captured 1 Field 9 Machine Gun	JAM
EPEHY	2/4	Held new outpost line in front of EPEHY - Casualties 2/Lt S E BOWDEN wounded OR 1 K, 1 S of W, 2 W. Relieved at dusk by 1/5th R War R. 2/Lt W H A Fisher joined for duty & C.W. graded C3. No 240276 Pte RICHMOND C.	JAM
GREBAUSSART WOOD	3/4	In support HQ & B & C Cos in GREBAUSSART WOOD - D Co in SAULCOURT WOOD. A Co attached 1/5th R War R	JAM
TEMPLEUX	4/4	Moved to Templeux into Bde Reserve - Reinforcement H.G.R	JAM
"	5/4	In Bde Reserve. Stood to at 6 a.m. in reserve for 145 Inf Bde who were attacking RONSSOY - LEMPIRE	JAM
"	6/4	In Bde Reserve	JAM
VILLERS FAUCON	7/4	Moved to VILLERS FAUCON. Working on roads	JAM

Army Form C. 2118.

WAR DIARY
or
INTELLIGENCE SUMMARY.

1/6 R War R

April 1917

(Erase heading not required.)

Instructions regarding War Diaries and Intelligence Summaries are contained in F.S. Regs., Part II. and the Staff Manual respectively. Title pages will be prepared in manuscript.

Hour, Date, Place		Summary of Events and Information	Remarks and references to Appendices
VILLERS FAUCON	8/4	In Div Reserve Welsh & Corps Inn	J & h
"	9/4	Attached to 48th Div H Q	J J h
"	10/4	"	J d h
"	11/4	Reinforcements 4 O.R	J L h
"	12/4	Capt J K Symes RAMC rejoined	J d h
	13/4	Left battalion front	J & h
PEIZIERE	14/4	Relieved 5th Lancashire Fusiliers on left battalion outpost line. A Co dug in four posts	
"	15/4	Reinforcement 4 O.R	J d h
"	16/4	Carried out a night attack into 5th R War R on right. Assault timed for 10 p.m. Terrible weather conditions. Objective gained on half the front. Capt J.N.G. STAFFORD & 2/Lt J HARRISON killed. Casualties O.R. 10 K 32 W. 2 Missing. Captured 1 Machine Gun	J d h
"	17/4	Relieved by 1/8th R War R. H.Q to CHAUFOURS WOOD. A 4 C Coys to SAULCOURT. B & D Coys attached 1/4 R War R & Div Reserve. Reinforcements arrived.	
CHAUFOURS WOOD	18/4		J d h
	19/4	In Div Reserve. Instructions in for 19th	Curly
		An	

B Buckham
Commandg 1/6 R War R

Army Form C. 2118.

WAR DIARY
or
INTELLIGENCE SUMMARY.
(Erase heading not required.)

Instructions regarding War Diaries and Intelligence Summaries are contained in F.S. Regs., Part II. and the Staff Manual respectively. Title pages will be prepared in manuscript.

Hour, Date, Place	Summary of Events and Information	Remarks and references to Appendices
CHAUFOURS WOOD D.20.d.3	bn Reserve. A Coy returned D Coy in EPEHY. Relieving men of Bat's Sector in front Posts from Coy of 1/6. R. War R. "D" by to SAULCOURT. "A" reinforcements to	cont.
21/4	Bat's moved to TEMPLEUX-LA-FOSSE	cont.
TEMPLEUX 22/4	2 Coys working on Roads, 2 Coys training.	cont.
23/4	Inspection by G.O.C. Division.	cont.
24/4	Training & work on Roads.	cont.
25/4	" " 5 reinforcements	cont.
26/4	MAJOR W.C.A. GENT took over temporary command.	cont.
27/4	Training & work on Roads.	cont.
28/4	do	cont.
29/4	Moved to billets in PERONNE. 2nd Lt W.B. COWAN 5th HANTS. and Lt S.G. SMITH, +2nd Lt R.W. FERRIDAY + 600 R. arrived to join the Batt.	cont.
PERONNE 30/4	Moved to FLUSIER AREA. Billets in Camp 50 bis.	cont.
	During the period under review the following Honours + awards were announced. 240167. Cpl. BOX. S.R. 243115. Sgt. RUBERRY. J.H. MILITARY MEDAL + UNT. J.	
	240165.	

Forms/C.2118/10

(9 29 6) W 4141—468 100,000 9/14 HWV

Operation Order No 4059a   No 2

Ref

50 C.S.F. 20,000   Lt. Col. by G Danielsen D.S.O.

1. The Battalion will take part in an attack on night of April 13/14th.

2. The 5th R. War R. are attacking on the right

3. The Battalion objective is the road running from X.28.a.9.9 to X.15.d.9.4.

4. Inter Company boundary Pigeon Ravine (inclusive to C Coy) – D Coy on right – C Coy on left.

5. Platoons 5 & 6 of B Coy are attached to D Coy. Platoons 7 & 8 of B Coy are attached to C Coy

6. A Coy holds present line and fetches rations & water (bringing petrol tins) when situation has quietened down.

7. Machine Guns of 143 M.G. Coy – one attached to D Coy to cover German outpost company about X.14.b.1.1 – one to C Coy to cover M.G. at X.15.c.5.9 – two to A Coy to cover above points and alternatively Pigeon & Quail Ravines.

8. Hour of assault 10 p.m. — assaulting troops will cross A Coy's line at 9.15 p.m.

9. Regimental aid post — S.W. of 14 Willows about F.1.b.4.4 — 8th Divn. also have one about X.25.a.1.8

10. Report centre — Head of Pigeon Ravine about X.21.c.6.4 — Advanced battalion H.Q. — 14 Willows X.26.a.5.0

11. Reserve of L.G. ammunition + S.A.A. at advanced battn. H.Q.

12. Artillery barrages have been fixed and communicated to all concerned

J.L. Mellor
Capt. & Adjt.
1/6th R. War. Regt.

Issued by hand 5.30 p.m.
16/4/17.

Additions to O.O. 40.

1. R.E.
A section of R.E. will be in cutting
X.25.a.9.4. and will help in consolidation
when sent up by order from Adv. H.Q.

2. Countersign
A man should challenge with the word
"Brummagem" and the answer should
be "Thorpe St."

3. Attack
The 145 Inf Bde are delivering an
attack on right of our brigade at 11.30 p.m.

J L Mellor
Capt & Adjt
1/6th R War Regt

16/4/17

A contact aeroplane will pass over
at 6.30 a.m. on 14th.

OPERATION ORDER NO* 59 By LIEUT. COL F.G.DANIELSEN, D.S.O.
COMMDG 1/6 R.WAR.REGT.   Copy No.....2...

Reference.   April 14th. 1917.
62c N.E. Ed. 3a.

1. The 1/6 R.War.Regt. will relieve the 5th. Bn. Lancashire Fusiliers in the Left Battalion Sector this evening.

2. Companies will move off in the following order: A,B,H.Qrs., C,D. Each half Company with 290 yards interval, 1st. half company to pass the H.Qrs. turning at 6-30 pm.

3. Guides from the 5th. Bn. Lancashire Fusiliers will meet the Battalion at the Marle Pit about E.6.a.8.4.

4. Dress: Fighting Order with greatcoats.

5. One limber per Coy. will proceed in the rear of each Coy. to carry Lewis Guns, Dicksies, cooking utensils and Officers' mess requirements. They are to report to Coys. at 6-0 pm.

6. Tool Limber will proceed in rear of A Coys. front half coy. and A & B Coys on reaching EPEHY will each draw 30 Shovels and 15 picks. The balance will be unloaded near Bn. HQrs. and be under the charge of the R.S.M.

7. One limber will report to Bn.HQrs. at 6-0 pm. and Maltese Cart will report at Aid Post at the same time. Both water carts will proceed in the rear of the Battalion.

8. Great care is to be taken that all waterbottles are filled before 2-0 pm. today.

9. Packs, with one blanket inside are to be taken to the Q.M. Stores at:

    A Coy. 3-0 pm. B Coy. 3-15 pm. C Coy. 3-30 pm.
    D Coy. 3-45 pm. H.Q. Coy. 4-0 pm.

                                        Capt.,
                              A/Adjutant, 1/6 R.War.Regt.
Issued by Order at 11-45 am.

Copy No. 1 File   Copy No. 8 Transport Officer.
 "   " 2 War Diary.   "   " 9 Adjutant.
 "   " 3 to 7 Companies.   "   " 10 Spare.

OPERATION NO. 60 BY LIEUT. COL. F.G.DANIELSEN, D.S.O.

COMMDG. 1/6 R.War.Regt.   Copy No. 2

Reference Sheet
62c N.E. Ed. 3a.   April 20th, 1917.

1. The 1/6 Bn. R.War.Regt. will be relieved on the morning of the 21st. by the 5th. Bn. East Lancs. Regt.

2. On relief, the Battalion will proceed to TEMPLEUX-LA-FOSSE.

3. D & C Coys. will each have 5 guides, Transport, Q.M.Stores and Bn. H.Qrs. one guide each detailed to report to 2/Lt. H.F.ALSOP at the Cemetery, SAULCOURT At 9-0 am. Bn. H.Q. will also detail a guide to take two companies to PIEZIERE. 5 Guides from B Coy and a Coy of the 1/8th. R.War.Regt will be at the Fork Rds. E5.d.8.6. at 9-30 a.m.

4. Dress: Full marching order carrying one blanket.

5. Companies will march independantly when relieved and proceed to TEMPLEUX-LA-FOSSE. Those moving from PIEZIERE must proceed with platoon intervals until passing through Saulcourt.

6. One limber will report at B Coys. H.Qrs. at 8-0 am. for Officers' Valises and all dixsies. At SAULCOURT and CHAUFFOUR WOOD all Officers', Mess Boxes, Lewis Guns etc.will be outside Battn and Coy. H.Qrs. at 8-30 am. Transport will be formed up in SAULCOURT and moved independently under the Transport Officer.

7. Billeting parties consisting of CQMSergts and 1 man from each platoon will report at the Q.M.Stores at 8-0 and move off to TEMPLEUX under the Senior CQMS when all are present. The party will meet the Adjutant at the Old Q.M.Stores, TEMPLEUX at 9-3P am

8. A limber will report to the 8th. R.War.Regt. H.Qrs. at 8 pm. and will proceed to a point ordered by the 8th. R.War.R. to pick up A Coys. Lewis Guns etc on relief.

                                            Captain,
Issued by Orderly at 5 pm.   Adjutant, 1/6 R.War.Regt.

Copy No. 1 File.   Copy No. 9 Transport Officer.
"   " 2 War Diary.   "   " 10 Adjutant.
"   3 to 7 Companies.
"   8   1/8 R.War.Regt.

OPERATION ORDER NO 81 BY MAJOR W.C.O.CELL, M.C., COMMDG. 1/6TH R.WAR.R.

Copy No........

28th April 1917.

1. The Battalion will move to PERONNE tomorrow. Companies will march in the following order with 200 yards between Coys., H.Qrs., D.C. B. A. Coys.

2. Coys. will fall in with the head of the leading Coy. outside Battalion Headquarters at 9.45 a.m.

3. Dress - Full marching order with great coat in pack and wearing steel helmet. Soft Caps will be strapped at the back of the valise.

4. Officers' kits and mess boxes, Lewis Guns and Blankets (tightly rolled in bundles of ten and clearly marked) will be dumped at entrance to camp by the cookers at 9.0 a.m. The Lewis Gun Officer will be responsible for the loading of the Lewis Guns and for providing a loading party for them. Battalion Headquarters' baggage will be outside Headquarters at 9.0 a.m.

5. Transport will be formed up ready to move at 9.45 a.m. with the head outside Q.M.Stores.

6. Dinners will be served on arrival.

7. Billeting party consisting of 2/Lt. Alsop, 4 Q.M.Sergts, Sgt. Dmr.Garvey, and one man per platoon will report to Battn. Headquarters at 8.0 a.m.

8. A. Coy. will provide a loading party of 1 N.C.O. and 6 men for loading the kits at 9.0 a.m.

9. Sick Parade will be at 8.30 a.m.

10. Officers' chargers will be at the various Headquarters at 9.30 a.m.

(Sd) C.W.CASSIEE, 2/Lieut.
A/Adjt., 1/6th R. War. Regt.

Issued by Orderly at 11.0 p.m.

Copy No 1. File.
    2. War Diary.
    3 to 7. Coys.
    8. T.O.
    9. Adjutant.

OPERATION ORDER NO 62 BY LT. COL. F.G.DANIELSEN, D.S.O., COMMDG.
1/6TH R. WAR. REGT.

Copy No.. 2......

April 29th 1917.

1. The Battalion will move to ECLUSIER Area tomorrow in the following order, Signallers, C. B. A. D. Coys. All other details will parade with their Companies.

2. Coys. will parade in the Square ready to move off at 10.15 a.m.

3. Dress - Full marching with great coat in pack and wearing steel helmet. All mess tins are to be carried inside the pack, and the soft caps strapped on the back thereof.

4. Officers' kits and mess boxes, Lewis Guns, will be dumped outside Battn. Headquarters at 9.0 a.m. 2/Lt. Grant will be responsible for the loading of the Lewis Guns, and B. Coy. will provide a loading party of 1 N.C.O. and 6 privates for the remainder at 9.0 a.m.

5. Transport will be formed up ready to move at 10.15 a.m. with the head facing road.

6. Dinners will be served on arrival.

7. Billeting party consisting of 2/Lt. Alsop and personnel as today will parade at Battn. Headquarters at 8.0 a.m. and move off to meet the Staff Captain at the Church, Eclusier at 10.30 a.m.

8. Leather Jerkins and Undercoats Fur will be collected by Coys. and tied securely in bundles of ten and five respectively, and will be returned to Ordnance, 48th Divnl. Dump, PERONNE, by 9.0 a.m. Those of the above collected by the Transport today will be disposed of in a like manner.

9. Blankets will dumped in the square, PERONNE by 9.0 a.m. B. Coy. will provide 1 N.C.O. and 3 men to stay with them as guard. These blankets will be conveyed to new area by lorry.

10. Officers' chargers to be at Battn. and Coy. Headquarters at 10.0 p.m.

11. Sick Parade will be at 7.0 a.m.

(sd) O.W.GASSETT, 2/Lieut.
A/Adjt. 1/6th R. WAR. REGT.

Issued by Orderly by 1.30 p.m.

Copy No 1. File.
2. War Diary.
3 to 7 Coys.
8. T.O.
9 Adjt.

Confidential.

War Diary of

1/6th Bn. R. War. R.

From 1st May 1917
To   31st May 1917

Army Form C. 2118.

WAR DIARY
or
INTELLIGENCE SUMMARY.
(Erase heading not required.)

Instructions regarding War Diaries and Intelligence Summaries are contained in F.S. Regs., Part II. and the Staff Manual respectively. Title pages will be prepared in manuscript.

Hour, Date, Place		Summary of Events and Information	Remarks and references to Appendices
ECLUSIER May 1st		Inspection of Coys.	
" " 2nd		Training + Sports and 2/Lts R.M.B.J. SOMERVILLE, H HALLAM	
PERONNE " 3rd		Moved to PERONNE. K.H. BULKLEY. Joined for duty Draft of # 14 O.R.	
" " 4th		Training	
" " 5th		do. 21 O.R. Joined	
" " 6th		Brigade Church Service.	
" " 7th		Training	
" " 8th		"	
" " 9th		"	
" " 10th		Working Parties	
" " 11th		Training	
LE TRANSLOY " 12th		Moved to LE TRANSLOY. added by III Corps Commander to FREMICOURT. Relieved 8th Batn Northumberlands	
in the Line " 13th		4 hrs. in outpost line in front of BOURSIES. A + C Coys in front line. B in support D in Reserve at Batn Hdqrs. with two platoons at Left Coy Hdqrs. A Coy on Right had posts Nos 1 - 7. C. Coy on left Nos 8 - 14.	
" 14th		Holding outpost line. Casualties O.R. killed 1. wounded 2	
" 15		do do do	
" 16		do do	
" 17		do Nil	
" 18		do B + D Coys relieved Coys in Front line. Casualties Nil. 2nd Lt. W.H. BEALE Joined. Draft of 6 O.R. do 6 O.R.	

(9 29 6) W 4141—463 100,000 9/14 H W V Forms/C. 2118/10

Army Form C. 2118.

WAR DIARY
or
INTELLIGENCE SUMMARY.
(Erase heading not required.)

Instructions regarding War Diaries and Intelligence Summaries are contained in F.S. Regs., Part II. and the Staff Manual respectively. Title pages will be prepared in manuscript.

Hour, Date, Place		Summary of Events and Information	Remarks and references to Appendices
In the line	May 19th.	Holding Outpost line. Casualties, wounded O.R.1.	enl.
	20.	do.	enl.
		A Coy attacked enemy post on CAMBRAI Rd. with two platoons. Conditions unfavourable, very dark night + misty. Post found to be strongly held + attack was fired off by heavy bomb + rifle fire. 2nd Lt. S.G. SMITH badly wounded in front few minutes of attack.	enl.
LEBUCQUIRE	21.	Battn relieved by 4th Gordons. 3 Coys to BEAUMETZ-MORCHIES line 1 Coy with Battn Hdqrs at LEBUCQUIRE. 3 Operations by Coys. Providing garrisons for BEAUMETZ-M. line	enl.
	22.	do.	enl.
	23.	Working parties wiring	enl.
	24.	do.	enl.
	25.	do.	enl.
	26.	do.	enl. on 26th enl.
	27.	do.	2nd Lt. H. BRADLEY joined. A R.S. ward Pioneers relieved. two Coys in BEAUMETZ-M. line on 26th enl. Third Coy relieved on above 27th enl.
	28.	do.	enl.
In the line.	29.	Relieved H9 Gdns in Rt Battn Sector. B + C in front line. A Coy Rt and D Coy Left Support. Casualties nil.	enl.
	30.	Holding Outpost Line.	2nd Lt. Q.H. SALMON joined. enl.
	31.	do.	enl.
		Honours + Awards. Major. W.M. PRYOR. D.S.O. Capt. M.A. LINFOOT. M.C. 240874. C.S.M. GOWDIE. M.C. 240504. Seqt. F. EASTHOPE. D.C.M. 240115. Seqt. J. HUNT. Bar to M.M. 241630. Cpl. TILLEY. M.M. Lcpl. HEATH. M.M. 241708 Pte. G.D. JONES. M.M.	enl.

(9 29 6) W 4141—463 100,000 9/14 H W V   Forms/C. 2118/10

CONFIDENTIAL.

WAR DIARY

of

6th ROYAL WARWICKSHIRE REGIMENT.

From 1st June to 30th June, 1917.

Army Form C. 2118.

WAR DIARY
or
INTELLIGENCE SUMMARY.
(Erase heading not required.)

Instructions regarding War Diaries and Intelligence Summaries are contained in F.S. Regs., Part II. and the Staff Manual respectively. Title pages will be prepared in manuscript.

Hour, Date, Place	Summary of Events and Information	Remarks and references to Appendices
In the line June 1.	Relieved 1/4 Glosters on Right Bn Sector	
" " 2.	Holding outpost line	
" " 3.	" " "	
" " 4.	" " " 2 wounded 1 nr cas	
" " 5.	" " " 11 Reinforcements	
Lesboeufs " 6.	Relieved by the Glosters moved to Lesboeufs	
" " 7.	Work of Posts, wiring & digging on trenches Beaulencourt line	
" " 8.	" " "	
" " 9.	" " "	
" " 10.	" " "	
" " 11.	" " "	
" " 12.	12 Reinforcements	
" " 13.	camp of aug 7	
" " 14.	" " "	
In line " 15.	Relieved the Glosters in outpost line	
" " 16.	Holding outpost line	
" " 17.	" " "	
" " 18.	A & D Coys attacked enemy front K.1 & 8/4 on Cambrai Rd. 10 B Coy. 1st Platoon each of C. Road D Coy. in support. Support Royal Tanks. Coop of Artillery. Barrage. MG Barrage. at Zero hour. White marked on Beaulencourt trenches	

Form/C. 2118/10

WAR DIARY
or
INTELLIGENCE SUMMARY.
(Erase heading not required.)

Army Form C. 2118.

Hour, Date, Place	Summary of Events and Information	Remarks and references to Appendices
June 18. continued	Platoon on left of Coy reached objective with few casualties but on the right they came under heavy barrage and were considerably fromed. Reinforcement by 2 Lts into machine objective was done 200 yards of road. 10 officers NCOs of enemy captured and considerable casualties inflicted. Our casualties Capt J. Linfoot, 2 Lts Grant and Dowsett wounded. 35 OR. wounded and 10 OR. missing.	AD
June 19	C.S.M. Gowdy and 3 OR. suffered by shell. D. Coy. under Capt. H.A. Linfoot searched ground near Ryves Cross Road for traces of enemy men. Rifle Craft and equipment encountered. Relieved in Craig line returned with 2 other casualties.	AD
20.	In line	AD
21.	"	AD
LE BUCQUIERE 22.	Relieved by 4th Seaforths. 2 Reinforcements	AD
FREMICOURT 23.	Spent day at Fremicourt.	AD
24.	"	
25.	12 Reinforcements. Lt Crook rejoined from hospital	

Army Form C. 2118.

WAR DIARY
or
INTELLIGENCE SUMMARY.
(Erase heading not required.)

Place	Date	Hour	Summary of Events and Information	Remarks and references to Appendices
GOMIECOURT.	30		Relieved by 7 Shropshire L.I. and marched to GOMIECOURT.	A.D.
			HONOURS AND AWARDS. Capt Mellor M.C. Capt Steffen mentioned in despatches. 2/Lt J. Roberts. Mentioned. C.S.M. Jones W. mentioned. Cpl. Nickless M.M.	A.D.

J.E. Davidson Lt Col
Commdg 1/6 RWK
30-6-1917

CONFIDENTIAL.

WAR DIARY
of

1/6th BN. ROYAL WARWICKSHIRE REGT.

From 1st July To 31st July, 1917.

Army Form C. 2118.

WAR DIARY
or
INTELLIGENCE SUMMARY.
(Erase heading not required.)

Instructions regarding War Diaries and Intelligence Summaries are contained in F. S. Regs., Part II. and the Staff Manual respectively. Title pages will be prepared in manuscript.

Army 1/4 Rear R.

Place	Date	Hour	Summary of Events and Information	Remarks and references to Appendices
Louvencourt Pommier	1st July		Brigade Church Parade.	N/a
	2nd		Marched to Pommier	N/a
	3rd		Training	N/a
	4th		do	N/a
	5th		do	N/a
	6th		do	N/a
	7th		Church Service 232 Reinforcements	N/a
	8th		Training Lt. Col. Davidson to England.	N/a
	9th		do	N/a
	10th		do Lt. W. H. Boyta joined for duty.	N/a
	11th		do 2nd Lieut. A. W. Wortelinge joined for duty. 17 Reinforcements	N/a
	12th		do	N/a
	13th		Church Parade. 2nd Lieut E. E. Andrew joined for duty. 3 Reinforcements	N/a
	14th		Training	N/a
	15th		do	N/a
	16th		do Lieut. Col. A. J. L. Mitchell took over command of the Bn.	N/a
	17th		do	N/a
	18th		do	N/a
	19th		do	N/a
Halloy	20th		Marched to Halloy	N/a
	21st		In Billets	N/a
	22nd		Marched to Authville, entrained for St. Jambu Riagen	N/a
St Jambu Riagen	23rd		Training	N/a
	24th		do	N/a
	25th		do	N/a
	26th		do	N/a
	27th		do	N/a

Army Form C. 2118.

WAR DIARY
or
INTELLIGENCE SUMMARY.
(Erase heading not required.)

Instructions regarding War Diaries and Intelligence Summaries are contained in F. S. Regs., Part II. and the Staff Manual respectively. Title pages will be prepared in manuscript.

Place	Date	Hour	Summary of Events and Information	Remarks and references to Appendices
St Jansha Ridge	28 July		Training	No.
	29 "		Church services.	No.
	30 "		Inspection of	No.
	31 "		marched into Corps reserve at Camp "C" A 30 d. Belgium Sheet 28 N.W.	No.

OPERATION ORDER NO.67 BY LT. COL. F.G.DANIELSON, D.S.O., T.D. COMDG*

1/6TH ROYAL WARWICKSHIRE REGIMENT.

Copy No........
~~29th June 1917.~~
1st July 1917.

1. The Battalion will move to-morrow to POMMIER.

2. Battalion will parade on Battalion Paradeground ready to march off at 8.30 a.m. Markers to report to R.S.M. at 8.30 a.m.

3. Order of march H.Qrs, B.C.D.A Coys. Transport will move in rear of Battalion.

4. Dress full marching order, Great Coats in Packs, wearing steel helmets All kits etc must be in haversacks or pack.

5. Officers kits and mess boxes to be dumped outside Battalion H.Q. not later than 7.15 a.m. "D" Coy. will provide a loading party for these at 7.15 a.m. consisting of one N.C.O. and 6 men.

6. Billeting party under 2Lt. H.F.Alsop of Q.M.S. Odell and 4 Coy Q.M.S. will parade at   the Orderly Room at 7.0 a.m. with Bicycles.

7. C.O's and 4 Coy. Commanders Chargers to be outside various H'Qrs at 7.30 a.m., remainder at 8.20 a.m.

8. Sick parade at 7.0 a.m.

9. Dinners wil be cooked on the road and served on arrival.

10. Distances of 500 yards between units and 200 yards between Coys. and section of Transport will be maintained.

11. Officers Commanding Coys will hand to the Adjutant before moving off a certificate that all billets and their Coy. area have been left in a clean and tidy condition.

12. Marching in states shewing number of men who fell out, mile and cause to be sent eto Orderly Room immediately on arrival.

(sd) A.N.Downing 2 Lt.
A/Adjutant 1/6th R.War Rgt.

No 1. File
2. War Diary
3.-7 5 Coys.
8. T.O.
9. Adjutant.

OPERATION ORDERS NO 68 BY LT.COL.A.J.N.BARTLETT, COMMANDING
1/6TH R. WAR. REGT.

Copy No.........

July 21st 1917.

1. The Battalion will move to AUTHIEULE tomorrow to entrain.

2. The Battalion will parade in the road running past H.Qrs. with the head of the column at the X roads in the following order H.Qrs. A. B. C. D. ready to move off at 2.15 a.m.

3. Transport will move in rear of the Battalion.

4. Dress - Full Marching Order with great coat in pack and wearing Steel Helmets.

5. Officers kits will be dumped outside Quartermaster's Stores at 9.0 p.m. tonight.

6. Mess Boxes. One mess box, for use during journey will be dumped outside Bn.H.Qrs. at 12.30 a.m. Remaining mess boxes to be carried on Cookers.

7. A. Coy. will detail 1 N.C.O. and 6 privates to be at Q.M. Stores at 9.0 a.m. for loading kits.

8. Tea will be served before moving off. Coy. Commander to arrange this leaving plenty of time for dixies to be cleaned.

9. Breakfast will be served at AUTHIEULE at 4.30 a.m.

10. The accommodation will be approximately one platoon to a truck and platoon Sergts. will be held responsible that no man leaves the train until the order is given.

11. 2/Lts Salmon & Wooldridge will Be Orderly Officers for the train, and will be responsible that N.C.O. or man leaves the train except at a recognised halt when the order will be given by the Commanding Officer. These Officers will be responsible for the right and left sides of the train respectively.

12. Coy. Commdrs. are responsible that their billets and area are left in a clean and tidy condition and they will hand a certificate to theisffeet this effect to the Adjutant when the Battn. parades.

13. H.Qrs. horses to be at Battn. H.Qrs. at 2.0 a.m.

(sd) A.N.Downing 2/Lt.
A.A.lt. 1/6th R. War. Regt.

SECRET.   Copy No.1......

1/6 TH ROYAL WARWICKSHIRE REGT.

OPERATION ORDER NO. 70.   JULY 30th/17.

Ref. map.
1/20.000 Sheet 28 N.W.
----

1. The Battalion, less Transport, will move to camps in wood,
    A 30.   on night 30th/31st July.

2. Coy. will parade outside their lines ready to move off at
    11.10 p.m.   Dress - Full Marching Order.

3. Route.- POPERINGHE, POPERINGHE-ELVERDINGHE Road, CHEMIN
    MILITAIRE.

4. Officer's kits and mess boxes will be stacked by cookers at 10.0 p.m.

5. Billiting party consisting of 2/Lt. H.F.Alsop, C.Q.M.S. and one
    from H. Qrs. will parade with Bicycles outside Orderly Room @ 3.30. p.m.

6. Coy. Officers will satisfy themselves that their lines have been
    left in a clean and tidy condition, and to report to the Adjutant
    that this has been done before moving off.

7. Distances of 500 yds. between units and 200 yds. between Coys. will
    be maintained.

8. The Transport will move under orders of the B.T.O.

                                    (sd) A. N. Downing.   2/Lieut.
                                       A/Adjt. 1/6th R. War. Regt.

No. 1. File.
    2. War Diary.
    3.- 7 5 Coys.
    8. T.O.
    9. Adjutant.

CONFIDENTIAL

WAR DIARY

of

1/6th ROYAL WARWICKSHIRE REGIMENT.

From 1st August,

To 31st August, 1917.

Army Form C. 2118.

WAR DIARY
or
INTELLIGENCE SUMMARY.
(Erase heading not required.)

Instructions regarding War Diaries and Intelligence Summaries are contained in F. S. Regs., Part II. and the Staff Manual respectively. Title pages will be prepared in manuscript.

Place	Date	Hour	Summary of Events and Information	Remarks and references to Appendices
Camp "C" A 30 d	Aug 1st		training	h.a.
	2nd		do	h.a.
	3rd		do	h.a.
	4th		do	h.a.
	5th		do	h.a.
	6th		do	h.a.
	7th		do	h.a.
	8th		moved to camp A 30 d 19	h.a.
Camp A 30 d 19	9th		training	h.a.
	10th		training	JH
	11th		training	JH
	12th		training	JH
	13th		training	JH
	14th		training	JH
	15th		Moved to Dambre Camp, march. Crossed Yser Canal moved forward in support East of the Steenbeke	JH
Dambre Camp St Julien Area	16th		West of the Steenbeke C 11 d 88. In support same position	JH
	17th			JH
	18th		2 & 3 Coys relieved 1/8 R.W. R. in Front line C 12 d 55 to C 12 d 28. Same position. Capt Chawl + 2/Lt Rhodes wounded. OR 1 Killed 14 Wounded. 2/Lt Woolley killed.	JH
	19th		Battalion relieved by 1/5 + 1/4 R. War. R. Army Forman Aug 16-20 m	JH
Regensburg Camp	20th		arrived Regensburg Camp 3 am	JH
	21st		training	JH
	22nd		training	JH
	23rd		training	JH
	24th		training	JH
	25th		training	JH
	26th		training	JH

Matthew Major
Commdg 1/6 R.War.R

Army Form C. 2118.

WAR DIARY
or
INTELLIGENCE SUMMARY.
(Erase heading not required.)

Instructions regarding War Diaries and Intelligence Summaries are contained in F. S. Regs., Part II. and the Staff Manual respectively. Title pages will be prepared in manuscript.

Place	Date	Hour	Summary of Events and Information	Remarks and references to Appendices
Reigersburg Camp St Julien Area	Aug 26 27		Moved into junction of N. & S. of St Julien - Wurmsey Rd. C.12.d 55 rdry in attacked at 1.55pm enemy position at Wurmsey farm Tanatiny C.12.d 80 and D.7.a.28. Advance unfavourable due to state of ground fire from M.G's & enemy in concrete emplacements. Capt Booker, 2/Lts Austin, Carrington killed. Capt. Partridge MC, 2/Lts Williams, M.Cg. Shearer wounded. 2/Lt Betts rich. O.R. Killed 25. O.R. Wounded 120 O.R. Missing 14.	J.H. J.H.
Reigersburg	28		Relieved by 1/4 Royal Berks about 10 a.m. Battalion assembled at Reigersburg Camp moved by train at 3 a.m. to Brown Camp, Elverdinghe	J.H.
Brown Camp S. Jansen Bergen	29 30 31		Marched to Junnelbery Camp, St Jansen Bergen. Training do	J.H. J.H. J.H.

majorly Major
Commanding H. H. Howard

SECRET.   Copy No............ 1.

1/6TH. ROYAL WARWICKSHIRE REGT.
OPERATION ORDER NO 72.

4/8/17

1. The 1/6th R. War. Regt. will move tomorrow to DAMERE Camp.

2. Coys. will fall in on their Coy. parade grounds in the following order, H.Qrs. A. B. C. D. Coys. ready to move off at 2.20 p.m.

3. Lewis Gun Limbers, Mess Cart, Maltese Cart, Tool Cart, Water Carts and Cookers will move in the rear of the Battalion.

4. Dress - Fighting Order.

5. Platoon Flags, grenades, tools &c. will be drawn at DAMERE Camp.

6. Officers' kits and mess boxes (with the exception of one box per mess) to be dumped in hut near Cookers by 1.15 p.m.
   One mess box and two sand bags per Coy. will be placed outside Q.M. Stores hut in camp ground by 1.45 p.m. to be put on mess cart.

7. Dinners will be at 12.0 noon.

8. Billeting party under 2/Lt. Alsop, consisting 4 C.Q.M.Sergts. and 1 N.C.O. from H.Qrs.., will parade outside Orderly Room at 11.0 am to proceed to take over camp.

9. O.C. Coys. will be responsible that the huts and the ground in the vicinity of their Billets are left clean & tidy.

10. Distances of 200 yards between Coys. will be maintained.

                                                    A. Downing
                                                         2/Lieut.
                                               a/Adjt. 1/6th R. War. Regt.

No. 1. File.
    2. War Diary.
    3-7 5 Coys.
    8   T.O. & Q.M.
    9. Adjutant
    10. Spare.

1/8th Batt. Royal Warwickshire Regt.
Operation Order No 71 Copy No 1
Preliminary Orders for move forward
from Present Area.   1/5/17

Ref Map Sheet 1/20,000 28 N.W.

1. The starting point is at A.30.d.19.
2. Battn will parade in the following order
Hd.Qrs. C. D. A. B Coys. Head of column to
be on road & to pass starting point at
zero + 35.

3. The following distances will be maintained
500 yds between units & 200 yds between
Coys.

4. Lewis Gun Limbers will move with Coy.
Maltese Cart with M.O. Cookers, Water &
Mess Cart will move under orders from
B.T.O. in rear of Brigade.

5. Rear half of L.G. Limbers to carry Lewis
Guns, Spare parts, & Ammn & with
the front half for Coy. Grenades.

6. Dress. - Fighting Order, each man carrying
4 Sandbags and (except bombers) one
extra bandolier of S.A.A.

7. Hot food will be served one hour before zero

8. Personnel not going into action will remain in present position until further orders

9. Packs will be stacked in the two huts of each Coy nearest the road & cookers. All packs must be marked with the name no. & platoon of the man in indelible pencil.

Brown
2/Lt & Adjt.

1/6 R Wark

Issued 4/7/30 pm
by orderly

Copies 1 & 2 War Diary
do 3 - 7 Coys
Copy 8 TO & QM
" 9 adjutant.

CONFIDENTIAL.

WAR DIARY.

of

1/6th ROYAL WARWICKSHIRE REGIMENT.

From 1st September,
To. 30th September, 1917.

* * * * * *

Army Form C. 2118.

WAR DIARY
or
INTELLIGENCE SUMMARY.
(Erase heading not required.)

September

Instructions regarding War Diaries and Intelligence Summaries are contained in F. S. Regs., Part II. and the Staff Manual respectively. Title pages will be prepared in manuscript.

Place	Date	Hour	Summary of Events and Information	Remarks and references to Appendices
ST. JAN TER BIELEN	1		Training 2/Lt. H.R. Willatt, A.L. Duckett, A.C. Green, 10/Cpmp. A.G. Thurrow, S. Rofers, W.F. Rex, J. Poyrton joined 30/8/17	
	2		Brigade Parade Church Service	
	3		Training	
	4		do	
	5		do	
	6		do	
	7		Lieut A.V. Brazier joined	
	8		Brigade Parade Church Service	
	9		Training	
	10		do	
	11		do — Capt C.E. Partridge joined	
	12		do	
	13		do	
	14		do	
	15		Brigade Parade Church Service	
	16		Batt. moved by march route to ABEELE Station Entrained at 9.0 a.m. Detrained	
LOUCHES	17		at AUDRICQ (Pas-de-Calais) Proceeded to LOUCHES by march route arriving at 3 p.m	
	18		Training 32 Other Ranks joined 1st Reinforcement from Base	
	19		do Lieut L.R. Couch joined	
	20		do 22 Reinforcements from 2/5th A & S. Highrs	
	21		do	
	22		do	
	23		Parade Church Service	
	24		Training 52 Reinforcements joined 2/R.E. Lycett	

Lieut Col
Comdg the Bn Black R/f.

Army Form C. 2118.

WAR DIARY
or
INTELLIGENCE SUMMARY.

(Erase heading not required.)

September

Place	Date	Hour	Summary of Events and Information	Remarks and references to Appendices
LOUCHES	25		Training	
	26		do	
	27		do + Brigade Sports	
	28		Training	
	29		do	
	30		Moved by March Route to ARBRUCQ Station. Entrained at 6.30 a.m. + detrained at VLAMERTINGHE + proceeded to DAMBRE Camp by march route arriving at 7.30 p.m.	
DAMBRE CAMP				
			Honours + Awards	
			Capt. R. S. Portroff Bar to M.C.	
			340003 C/Sjt. Bishop C.J. D.C.M.	
			310137 L/C. C.A.Orson M.M.	
			265542 Pte. H. Bean M.M.	
			310638 W. Jones M.M.	
			310098 A/Sjt. R. Gore M.M.	
			310456 Pte. J. Sutton M.M.	

Signed...
Commanding 16 Battalion

OPERATION ORDER BY LT. COL. W.M.PRYOR D.S.O. COMMANDING

1/6TH ROYAL WARWICKSHIRE REGIMENT.

Copy No........
29th. Sept. 1917

1. The Battalion will entrain tomorrow at AUDRUICQ to move to DAMPRE CAMP.

2. The Battalion will parade with head of column ready to move off outside Hd. Qrs. Mess at 6.45 a.m. in the following order,- Hd. Qrs., A. B. C. Coys. "D" Coy will join at the rear of the column as the column marches passed their billets.

3. Dress Full Marching Order.

4. Officers Kits and Mess Boxes will be dumped in Orderly Room yard by 6.0 a.m. Mens packs will be stacked in Companies on the side of the road near Orderly Room by 5.30 a.m.

5. "A" Coy will detail a loading party of 1 N.C.O. and 20 men for loading lorries and will report to Orderly Room at 6.15 a.m.

6. Billeting party under 2Lt. Trickett of 4 C.Q.M.Sergts. and 1 N.C.O. from Hd. Qrs will parade outside Orderly Room at 2.30 a.m. They will proceed by the first Personnel Train and will report to Lt. Walker at the detraining station.

7. 2Lt. Willatt will act as Entraining Officer and will report to Staff Capt. at AUDRUICQ at 8.30 a.m. He will obtain from the Orderly Room an entraining state which he will hand to the R.T.O.

8. Breakfast at 5.0 a.m.

9. Transport will proceed by train departing at 3.0 p.m. They will arrive at Entraining Station 3 hours before the train is ready to depart.

10. Officers Chargers and Mess Cart to proceed with the Column and to wait at entraining station for the Transport.

11. Officers Commanding Coys will see that their Billeting Areas are left thoroughly clean.

(sd) A.N. Downing 2Lt. & A/Adj.
1/6th R. War. Regt.

No. 1.File
2. War Diary
3-7 5 Coys.
8.T.O.
9 Adjutant.

CONFIDENTIAL.

W A R   D I A R Y

of

1/6th   ROYAL WARWICKSHIRE REGIMENT.

From 1st October,
To 31st October, 1917

WAR DIARY or INTELLIGENCE SUMMARY

Army Form C. 2118.

(Erase heading not required.)

October 1917

Place	Date	Hour	Summary of Events and Information	Remarks and references to Appendices
Hambre Camp	1			
"	2		CO 2nd i/c Adj O/C went forward & reconnoitred positions for the attack the night of 1/2 and 2/3. Balance of assembly positions.	
Canal Bank	3		Lt Henly Brown at 4.30 PM for the Canal Bank. 1st Bn 1st/2nd/3rd Platoons Coy. Platoon Sjts. accompanied assembly trenches. The following Offrs were wounded Wm Garrett, 2/Lt Boc + Mr Green, also P3 Platoon Sjts.	
Assembly Trenches	4		5.30 PM. 1st & 3rd moved up, relieved 4th R & BLI in the line. At 5.30 AM attacked. The attack was extremely successful, all objectives being taken except Bihn House + Vicken Farm extremely Prisoners captured 350, MGs 10, Aust. Tank Guns 2. Casualties. Officers killed, Capt AV Bidester, Capt HS Powell MB. 2/Lt Hallam, 2/Lt Poynton, 2/Lt Hussey. 2/Lt Tokey. Wounded Capt Musgrave, 2/Lt Hearne. Capt Knickett, 2/Lt Collins, 2/Lt Thurman.	
Advanced Positions	5		Other Ranks. Killed 28 Missing 32 Wounded 153 — 1st Held new line	
"	6		8 PM: relieved by 1/8 R.W.R in front line. Batt'n going back in reserve in the Langemarck line	
Langemarck Line	7			
"	8		9 PM moved back into Divisional Reserve at Irish Farm	

Army Form C. 2118.

WAR DIARY
or
INTELLIGENCE SUMMARY.
(Erase heading not required.)

October 1917

Instructions regarding War Diaries and Intelligence Summaries are contained in F. S. Regs., Part II. and the Staff Manual respectively. Title pages will be prepared in manuscript.

Place	Date	Hour	Summary of Events and Information	Remarks and references to Appendices
Proby Camp	9		About midday moved to Siege Camp. Reinforcements 1/50	
Siege Camp	10		21 OR S.C. brigm. 5/Seaforths & Winchester authorities of Gunners	
			Moved to Poperinghe, Entrained at 10 PM 2/Lt OD Billups joined	
Poperinghe	11		Training	
"	12		— 3 Reinforcements 7/50 OR Bullen joined	
"	13			
"	14		Moved by rail from Peselhoek to Mont St Eloi	
Mont St Eloi	15		Training	
"	16		Moved into the line, relieving the 25 Canadian Bgn Bns	
In the line	17		2/Lt Esmielle + 30 other rank wounded (SW)	
"	18		3 other ranks joined	
"	19		4 do do	
"	20		2/Lt J Rhodes regimental & other ranks joined	
"	21		4 Other ranks joined	
"	22			
"	23			
"	24			
"	25			
"	26			
"	27		2 Other ranks joined	
			Relieved by the 1/5 KR Staffs R & moved to Fraser Camp.	
Mont St Eloi	28		A.S.C. recruits training, remainder working on Winnipeg Camp	6 OR joined
	29			
	30			
	31		— Cubit Camp	

Whitehead
Commanding Battalion

SECRET.   Copy No...2......

1/6TH ROYAL WARWICKSHIRE REGT.

OPERATION ORDER. No 74a.   13rd Oct. 1917.

1. The Battalion will entrain tomorrow at PESELHOEK to proceed to 1st Army area.

2. The Battalion will parade with head of column, ready to move off, outside C. Coy's billet at 1.15 a.m. in the following order - H.Qrs, A. B. C. & D. Coys.

3. Dress - Full Marching Order.

4. Officers kits and mess boxes will be dumped in Q.M.Stores by 9.30 p.m. tonight.

5. Blankets will be rolled in bundles of 10 and dumped in Q.M.Stores by 4.0 p.m. this afternoon. A. Coy. will detail a loading party of 1 N.C.O. and 20 men for loading lorries, they will report at Q.M.Stores at 10.30 p.m. tonight.

6. 2/Lt Willatt will act as Battn. Entraining Officer. He will report to Capt. Bushell, Bde Entraining Officer, at PESELHOEK Station at 12.30 a.m. He will obtain from the Orderly Room an entraining state which he will hand to the R.T.O.

7. Transport will proceed with Unit and will report at entraining station at 12.30 a.m.

8. Rations for the 14th will be issued before moving off, and a hot meal will be served at 9.0 p.m.

10. Distances of 100 yards between Coys. will be maintained.

11. O.C.Coys. will see that their Coy. billets are left thoroughly clean.

                                        (sd) A.N.DOWNING, Lieut.

                                        A/Adjt. 1/6th R. War. Regt.

No 1. File.
   2. War Diary.
   3 - 7 5 Coys.
   8. T.O. & Q.M.
   9. Adjutant.

Operation Order No. 74 by Lieut Col Lowe Major DSO
Comm'dg 1/6 Bn R.Wark.   Copy No. 2
Ref Sheet: POELCAPELLE 2nd Ed 1/10,000   October 2/17.

1. The ~~Batln~~ Brigade will attack in conjunction with New Zealand Brigade on Right & 3rd Infy Bde on Left.
   Zero hour will be notified later.

2. Forming up positions. Battn will form up on taped lines already reconnoitred — in following order:—
   Right front — A Coy
   "   Rear — C
   Left front — D
   "   Rear — B

3rd Objectives A Coy 1 Platoon — Stoke Farm
                       2 Platoons — WINCHESTER & (melros's)
                                    on Stroombeck at D.1.d.99
                       1 Platoon — Reserve.

The detailed platoon for STOKE will be prepared to assist the 5th Bn R.Wark. to capture Concrete Structure at D.2.a.9.510 if required after the capture of STOKE.

A Coy will consolidate on red dotted line —
1 Platoon at WINCHESTER — 1 Platoon at STOKE and 2 platoons to be withdrawn to position behind STOKE to act as Battn reserve with 2 platoons of D Coy.

The strong point at WINCHESTER will be sited with centre main post and two flank posts.

D Coy 2 Platoons post at D.1.b.9.1. and YORK on to level with WINCHESTER according to take it if required.

D Coy Objectives Contd.   Page 2

1 platoon dotted red line 100 yds to left of YORK
1 platoon — reserve
One platoon detailed for YORK will assist A Coy to capture 3 mebus's at D1 d 9.9.

D Coy will consolidate with 2 posts on dotted red line & 2 platoons withdrawn to behind WINCHESTER to act as Battn reserve with 2 platoons of A Coy.

C Coy
2 platoons — Coy frontage up to red line.
1 platoon — To assist 5th Bn R. loan R. by attacking WELLINGTON from N.
1 platoon — Reserve.

Left leading platoon to assist in capture of concrete emplacement at V 26 d 4.2. Coy will consolidate on red line. It will join up with 5th Bn R. loan R. at D 2 b 6.8. & form 2 posts on Coy frontage along line of old trenches. Remainder of Coy will be distributed in depth behind.

1 platoon will be organised & brought up behind protective barrage ready to occupy VACHER FARM when protective barrage lifts at Zero + 5 hours.

B Coy
2 platoons at concrete emplacements at D 2 a 4.5.60 and occupied trenches about D 2 a 8. then concrete emplacements at V 26 d 4.2.
1 Platoon BURNS HOUSES
1 do RESERVE
Coy will consolidate — 1 platoon — 2 M.G's at BURNS HOUSES — 1 platoon V 26 d 4.2

(8) B Coy Objectives Contd.   Page 3

2 platoons trenches about D2a88. Strong point will be made at BURNS HOUSES 2 M.G.s are detailed for this point.

(3) A. Reserve The 4 platoons reserve - to be withdrawn from A & D Coys - will be under the orders of the C.O. They will however be used to resist a Counter-attack if required by Coy Commders without reference to Bn HQ which will however, be immediately informed of action taken.

Machine Guns. On capture of first objective, No 3 M.G. Coy will bring up 4 M.Gs. to WINCHESTER FARM, on capture of 2nd objective 2 guns to BURNS House.

4. As soon as possible (probably after dark) the 5/6/7th Bns R. War R. will take over the front line from the 6th & 8th Bns R. War R. as far back as the dotted red line. The 6th Bn will continue to hold strong points at WINCHESTER, STOKES & YORK FARMS. Remainder of Bn will then assemble in artillery formation in dead ground behind STOKE & WINCHESTER Farms. It will constitute a Brigade Reserve to be used in case of Counter attack.

5. Equipment Fighting Order with packs.
        Packs will contain Water Bottle
                            Tube Helmet
                            One day's rations
                            Iron rations
                            Oil sheet
                            & Nothing Else.

4. Equipment Cont'd   Page 4

Every man will carry 1 No 23 bomb in his pocket.
Rifle Grenadiers will carry two No 23 bombs & 6
blanks & rods.

Aeroplane flares. Every man will carry 1 tin
containing two flares, in his pocket.

Tools. 1 man per section will carry a shovel.
(Strong men will be detailed for this).

Tommy Cookers &
Stock - Bouillon } will be carried as issued to Coys

S.O.S Signals. 1 Lamp per Coy will be carried.

Message Rockets. 2 per Coy will be carried

6. Batt. H.Q.s will be at HÜBNER FARM – advanced Bn Hq
will be at WINCHESTER FARM when taken.

7. Regimental Aid Post at MON DU HIBOU
   5 Bn R Wark Aid post at JANET FARM.

8. Liason. Flank Coys will maintain connection with
Coys Battalions on right & left.

9. Barrage will be as per barrage map Shown to Coy
Officers. The following points will be known to
enable attacking troops to get up on the flanks
   WINCHESTER FARM – Emplacement at V26d42
   VACHER FARM

                              A Dawe
                              Lieut
                    A/Capt 1/6 Batt R War Regt

Copy No 1 File
       2 War Diary
       3 O.C A Coy
       4   " B "
       5   " C "
       6   " D "
       7   " Office
       8   " do

SECRET.   Copy No:.........

1/6TH BN. ROYAL WARWICKSHIRE REGT.

OPERATION ORDER NO. 75.   15/10/17.

1. The Battn. will relieve the 26th Canadian Inf. Regt. tonight the 15th inst.

2. The Battn. will parade ready to move off at 4.50 p.m.

3. Dress as already ordered.

4. Distances of 200 yards between Coys. will be maintained after detraining.

5. O.C. Coys. will report relief complete to Battn. H.Qrs. in the following code words - "rations delivered".

6. Coys. will render copies of Trench Stores taken over to Battn. H.Qrs. as soon as possible after relief.

7. Officers Trench kits and one mess box per Coy. to be dumped at Q.M.Stores at 2.0 p.m. for conveyance by limber. Officers valises and remainder of stores to be dumped at Q.M.Stores before moving off.

8. O.C.Coys. will ensure that all billets and camp ground are left in a clean state. Particular attention will also be paid to sanitation in the line.

                              (sd) A.P. DOWNING, Lieut.

                              A/Adjt. 1/6th R. War. Regt.

No 1. File.
   2. War Diary.
   3 - 7 Coys.
   8. O.C. D.H.Q.
   9. Adjutant.
  10. 2SO.rc.

143/48

1/5 R. Warwick Regt
Feb 1916
Vol XII

12 T.
(intact)

$\frac{143}{48}$

1/6 R. Warwick Regt

Vol XI

January 1916.

www.ingramcontent.com/pod-product-compliance
Lightning Source LLC
Chambersburg PA
CBHW080853230426
43662CB00013B/2092